Freud and the Child Woman

Freud and the Child Woman

The Memoirs of Fritz Wittels

Edited with a preface and commentary by
Edward Timms

Yale University Press
New Haven and London   1995

Set in Bembo by SX Composing Ltd, Rayleigh, Essex
Printed and bound in Great Britain by St Edmundsbury Press

Library of Congress Catalog Card Number 95–21047

ISBN 0–300–06485–3

A catalogue record for this book is available from the British Library.

Frontispiece: Fritz Wittels, outside his New York consulting room at
91 Central Park West, at the time when he began to write his memoirs.

Contents

Illustrations

Permission to reproduce illustrations from the following sources is gratefully acknowledged:

Abraham Brill Library, New York: **47**, **48**; *Adolf Loos: Das Werk des Architekten*, ed. Heinrich Kulka: **26**; Archiv Dr Christian Brandstätter, Vienna: **9**; Basic Books, New York: **16**; Bildarchiv des Instituts für die Geschichte der Medizin, Vienna: **10**; Bildarchiv der Österreichischen Nationalbibliothek, Vienna: **4**, **5**, **13**, **21**, **22**; Culver Pictures, Inc.: **27**; Edward Timms Archive, University of Sussex: **19**, **30**; Freud Museum, London: **35**; Fritz Wittels Collection, University of Sussex: frontispiece, **8**, **15**, **32**, **36**, **37**, **38**, **39**, **40**, **41**, **42**, **43**, **44**, **46**; Historisches Museum der Stadt Wien: **2**, **17**, **25**; Jarrolds Publishers, London: **29**; Library of Congress, Washington: **31**; Liveright Publishing Corporation, New York: **33**, **34**; Österreichisches Theater-Museum, Vienna: **3**; Sigmund Freud Copyrights: **28**, **45**; Sigmund-Freud-Haus-Archiv, Vienna: **7**, **11**; Universitäts-Verlag Wilhelm Braumüller, Vienna: **1**, **6**; Verlag Die Fackel, Vienna: **12**, **14**, **18**, **24**; Verlag Julius Zeitler, Leipzig: jacket design, **23**; Wiener Stadt- und Landesbibliothek, Vienna: **20**.

Editor's Preface

It was a chance conversation in a Hampstead coffee-house with Peter Gay, Freud's most recent biographer, that led me to the papers of Fritz Wittels.[1] I had become interested in Wittels while researching the relationship between Freud and Karl Kraus, but my first impressions were by no means favourable. Wittels, I wrote in *Karl Kraus: Apocalyptic Satirist* (New Haven and London, 1986), 'was essentially a popularizer of other people's ideas' (p. 99). At the same time, however, I identified him as a pivotal figure who, by linking the circles of Kraus and Freud, contributed to the cross-fertilization between different disciplines which was such a feature of Viennese culture around 1900. After reading a wider range of Wittels's writings, including unpublished material in archives in Vienna and London, I became aware that he could also be regarded as a significant figure in his own right and that his career might reward further study. Sitting at my desk in Cambridge, England, I gradually began to identify with Wittels and to ask myself what I would have done if I had been in his position in New York in the 1940s, a successful psychoanalyst nearing the end of my career, looking back on the days when I was privileged to be a member of the intimate circle not only of Karl Kraus but also of Sigmund Freud. What would I have done if I were Wittels? – I would have written my memoirs!

When I mentioned this possibility to Peter Gay after a morning spent at the Freud Museum in Hampstead, he suggested that it would be worth paying a visit the A. A. Brill Library in New York. Guided by this kind suggestion as well as my own intuition, I shortly afterwards flew to New York and gained access to Fritz Wittels's posthumous papers, which had indeed been deposited in the Brill Library. No words can describe my delight at discovering that the memoirs which I had conjured up in my imagination actually existed – amid a copious collection of other unpublished typescripts. For the memoirs, written in English during the early 1940s, provide unique insights into the bohemian subculture of Freud's Vienna. Indeed, they shed an unexpected light not only on the subversive activities of Kraus's coffee-house circle, but also on the supposedly scientific pursuits of the Vienna Psychoanalytic Society.

Fritz Wittels was born in Vienna in 1880 and died in New York in 1950. He was a prolific author of both psychoanalytic and literary works, but he is best known as Freud's first biographer. His book *Sigmund Freud: His Personality, His Teaching and His School* was published in English translation in London in 1924, having appeared in German at the end of the previous year. This is a first-hand account of Freud's early career, written by one of the early members of the Vienna Psychoanalytic Society. At the time of publication the book provoked considerable controversy, since it criticized certain authoritarian tendencies in Freud's personality, while at the same time praising the work of his rival, Wilhelm Stekel. However, its full significance only becomes apparent when it is compared with his alternative account of the early history of psycho-analysis – the personal memoirs which he wrote in English in New York under the provisional title 'Wrestling with the Man: The Story of a Freudian'.

The fact that these memoirs have been gathering dust in the archives for so many years raises a number of important questions. The most obvious puzzle is why a document of such importance should have remained unpublished for so long. One answer is suggested by a handwritten note found among Wittels's papers, probably written by his widow Poldi Goetz Wittels. After her husband's death she evidently tried to find a publisher for the memoirs, only to be told that they could not be published for fear of upsetting 'Jehovah's children'. Since Wittels, taking issue with Freud's authoritarian tendencies, refers in his memoirs to Freud's alleged 'Jehovah complex', this is evidently a reference to loyal disciples who wished the great man's authority to remain unchallenged. They would have been outraged (perhaps they still will be) by the frankness with which Wittels writes about the early controversies in which Freud and his followers were involved, particularly the scandal involving the second of Wittels's two 'spiritual fathers', the satirist Karl Kraus. For the memoirs reveal that during the first decade of the twentieth century the investigations of the Vienna Psychoanalytic

Society were closely entwined with the Viennese *demi-monde*, not least with the problematic erotic cults surrounding the 'child woman', Irma Karczewska.

During the lifetime of the main protagonists, the intriguing story of Irma's interactions with Kraus, Wittels, Freud, Stekel and other members of the Vienna Psychoanalytic Society remained a closely guarded secret, despite the controversies and court cases in which some of them became involved. Only once, during the mid-1920s, did investigative journalists come close to uncovering the identity of the 'child woman'. This was when the staff of the Viennese daily newspaper *Die Stunde*, at the height of their controversy with Kraus, began to probe the secrets of his private life. It so happens that one of the journalists working for *Die Stunde* was the young Billy Wilder, later to become a celebrated Hollywood film director. Although Wilder's early experiences in Vienna are not well documented, he too was involved in the campaign against Kraus and may possibly have stumbled on the Irma Karczewska story. Could this perhaps be one of the original sources for his celebrated film about a golden-hearted prostitute, *Irma La Douce*?

Since it was Wittels who in 1907 initiated the cult of the 'child woman', in a paper which he read to Freud in private, presented to the Psychoanalytic Society and then published in Kraus's magazine *Die Fackel* ('The Torch'), it is appropriate that he should finally reveal the underlying circumstances. It is, however, a matter for regret that he was not able to ensure that his memoirs were published in the form he wished. Fifty years after their composition, it is difficult to reconstruct his precise intentions, particularly as the typescript, originally entitled 'Wrestling with the Man', is at certain points incomplete. Moreover Wittels also left behind three draft chapters for a second volume, to be entitled 'When Vienna was Vienna: Reminiscences of a Former Resident'. Under these circumstances the editor (with the kind consent of the author's son, John R. Wittels) has taken the liberty of conflating these two sources, reshaping Wittels's typescript so as to produce a coherent narrative. To avoid repetition, certain sections have had to be compressed. But no cuts have been made in the substance of the text, apart from digressions about the history of Vienna, which Wittels acknowledges to be 'a hobby which the reader probably does not share'. At some points the sequence of the episodes has been altered so that the chronology becomes more coherent, and the chapter headings have also been revised to give a clearer overall picture. In addition, a new title has been chosen which brings out more clearly the essential theme of the book. Wittels's typescript reveals that he considered a number of alternative titles without being entirely satisfied with any of them. Initially he intended to call the book 'Ambivalence as Fate' or 'A Story of Ambivalence', but decided against this because he felt that the concept of ambivalence would not be understood. His final preference was for the biblical phrase 'Wrestling with the Man', which he felt would be more familiar to readers in the 1940s. For readers in the 1990s, however, it is the biblical reference which is likely to prove puzzling. The editor, in consultation with John R. Wittels, has opted for an entirely new title, *Freud and the Child Woman: The Memoirs of Fritz Wittels*.

Further details of the policy adopted in preparing this edition for the press are given in the Commentary at the end of the book. The editor has seen it as his brief to produce a readable text from the rather incoherent typescripts, not simply to correct spelling mistakes or insert missing commas. Although this has involved some restructuring of the narrative, great care has been taken to retain the vigour of Wittels's style. His English has been amended where the meaning is unclear or where his penchant for short sentences might produce a staccato effect. Further changes have been made to correct factual errors and the occasional solecisms of a writer whose mother-tongue was German. In the case of Wittels's translations of German texts, however, particularly his English versions of letters received from Freud, no changes have been made even when they read rather oddly, since the mistranslations may themselves be of interest.

The most significant changes are noted in the Commentary, which also incorporates Notes on the Text designed to clarify the context to which the memoirs refer. Drawing on wide-ranging research into the cultural history of Vienna, including the personal testimony provided by Wittels's love letters to Irma Karczewska and Irma's own unpublished diary, the Notes elucidate some of the more cryptic details alluded to in the memoirs. Wittels's aim was to write a subjective personal memoir, not a comprehensive autobiography. The further sources and documents cited may provide a more balanced picture of one of the most colourful and controversial figures in the early history of psychoanalysis. A series of illustrations have also been incorporated to enhance these personal reminiscences of the culture of Vienna in its golden age.

Introduction by Fritz Wittels: Wrestling with the Man

> And Jacob was left alone; and there wrestled a man with him until the breaking of the day . . .
> And he said, Let me go, for the day breaketh. And he said, I will not let thee go, except thou bless me . . .
>
> (Genesis 32: 24, 26)

I met Freud in 1905. Six years later, in 1911, I had a quarrel with him resulting in a severance of our personal relations, a rupture which, though lasting for a number of years, was never complete. Only a few people know why for some time I lived apart from the central light of psychoanalysis, and these few are diminishing rapidly in number, death harvesting substantially among them. Meanwhile, times have changed, and I feel that our ancient feud cannot be told to the present generation without a detailed explanation. To understand fully both the circumstances of the breach and the personal touch behind it, it is important to reconstruct something of the spiritual life of Vienna around 1910, a spirit not in existence any longer – no longer in existence even before its ultimate destruction by Hitler. This may sound like a deterrent: why rake up old stories? I feel, however, a strong stimulus deriving from the very difficulty of conjuring up that Athens on the Danube where we lived. We ourselves formed part of it, part of the old Austrian culture in which Freud was rooted, like myself, and which both of us outgrew: he in gigantic dimensions and I in his shadow.

I know that by saying so I give offence to his older and more orthodox disciples. They will recognize a haughty presumption in this juxtaposition of Freud and myself – an *identification*, as it is called in our terminology. All of his disciples identify with Freud. They are not aware of this mechanism within themselves, but at the same time they are very sharp-eyed in discovering and

disliking it in other people. Some of them imitate his
handwriting, some round up their speech or their gestures in his
way, shake hands as he did, or occasionally hold an index finger
at the upper front teeth as he sometimes did after the operation
on his jaw. More valuable than all these things would be an
identification with his way of thinking. But even here it is
imperative to distinguish between blind repetition of his
principles and free continuation of his artistic science. There is a
borderline between hypnotic bondage on the one hand and
constructive emancipation from the shackles of an over-
whelming spirit on the other.

My own identification with Freud is not with his person, at
least not any more, and not a blind dependency on his scientific
framework either. All of us must at some time wrestle with the
demon or the angel, and none comes out of the struggle without
a scar. But I hope that I now understand psychoanalysis
sufficiently well to use it in freedom. I identify with Freud in the
Viennese culture of the nineteenth century which we share.
Although it was several decades later than he that I walked
through the lecture halls of the Vienna medical school, and over
a quarter of a century later that I sat in Vienna's Burgtheater and
read the editorials of the liberal papers, it was still the same
Austria in which Freud grew up. The same light, declining but
yet bright, still shone; there was perceptible the same slight smell
of decay, and there could be felt the sensation as of a dull
shaking of the ground on which we stood – the signs of the birth
pangs of a new era and glimpses of the promised beauty of a
new life which, to this day, has failed to be born. I belong to
Freud's generation and my identification with him lies in this
fact. The years between his birth and mine may permit me to
lift myself somewhat above the wreckage of the nineteenth century and thereby enable me to tell the generation after me how it
was. I understand the new language, although I do not speak it
very well.

Freud was a modern man, one of the pioneers who helped
powerfully to set the foundations of the time in which we live.
Yet there was in his behaviour some of the Old-Austrian dignity
and courtesy which our time hardly understands any longer. It is
indeed difficult to explain to others what kind of a civilization
perished with the First World War, its traces eradicated by the
subsequent Nazi invasion. One thing is certain: it can never
return. Many hundreds of years were needed for its slow building up; a brief time of brutal power was sufficient to destroy it.

Where is the city of Baghdad, destroyed by the Moguls? Where is the city of Mozart, Beethoven, and Freud?

Originally, I meant to call the book, when finished, 'Ambivalence as Fate'. In Vienna, indeed throughout the Habsburg Monarchy, they used to speak half in jest and half in earnest of 'an expert Austrian' ['ein gelernter Österreicher']. Since psychoanalysis has introduced the concept of 'ambi-valence', it is easy to say what was meant by the phrase 'an expert Austrian', namely, a man who simultaneously loved and hated his country.[1] Ambivalence is widespread among men, indeed, it is fairly universal. An Austrian, however, had to be master of 'one auspicious and one dropping eye'.[2] During the First World War, just after a decisive victory over the Russians by the Central Powers, I ran across the playwright Arthur Schnitzler, one of the foremost 'expert Austrians'.[3] He said to me: 'You know how much I hate everything in Austria, yet when I heard that the danger of a Russian invasion was over, I felt like kneeling down and kissing this soil of ours'. This is ambivalence, and much of it will come to life in the pages that follow.

1

Childhood in Vienna

My mother died in 1887 when I was six years old, and I cannot even remember how she looked.[1] I have a photograph of her which depicts a young woman with classic features and a distinctive air, dressed in the fashion of the early eighties, which impresses us today as the style of a bygone epoch. The face is that of a stranger to me. In this sense my early development diverged widely from that of Freud, whose mother died in 1931 in her ninety-sixth year, when he was seventy-five.

In his study of Leonardo, Freud identifies the Mona Lisa's smile as an expression habitual on the face of Leonardo's mother, which came back to the artist as a recollection after his fiftieth year, the recall of an early childhood memory.[2] Freud himself had reached this same age when he wrote this study, and the question arises: what part did the investigator's own personal experiences contribute to this paper and in what ways did they determine so many other theories? What prepared Freud, we wonder, for those psychological discoveries which he continued to make for so many years with an almost somnambulistic certainty, even after he had gathered about him a considerable number of collaborators? We may well assume that specific individual experiences played their part in this. Freud once hinted something of the sort in a letter to me, as though he knew that some explanations were to be expected after his death. Before leaving Vienna, however, he burned almost all his notes, and although I always hoped that we would some day learn more of this, there is little hope now left of understanding this question.

How does a man see femininity who lost his mother in his early years, and how a man who kept her until his old age? One would think that, because of the tremendous significance of the mother and the mother role to the individual, two fundamentally different pictures must result; so different that, in a way, they might even resemble each other. I do not mean to be paradoxical, but as an experienced psychoanalyst I know that contrasts often mean the same: *les extrèmes se touchent*. One thing is certain: both pictures differ from that of a normal son who loses his mother when grown but not yet quite old. The one has imbibed too much, the other not enough of that stuff which first flows from the mother's breast and later continues as affection, guidance and, at times, coercion. These influences are not easily described in words.

The psychology of femininity, it seems to me, was until lately a stepchild of psychoanalysis. One may trace this to the inhibitions which love and awe placed about the figure of an ageing mother and which veiled the usual sagacity of Freud when he turned in this direction. My own relation to femininity will be discussed later and compared with Freud's concepts. Since I have myself been analysed, I feel a distinct mental darkness whenever the early loss of my mother creeps in. Neurotic men often suffer from too much mother and almost as frequently from too little mother. I believe I can understand both of them, but I am more closely touched by those who complain of too little.

When my loss occurred, I did not have the feeling of a loss; perhaps it would be better to say that I have no recollection of such a feeling. On a certain morning, which must have been 11 January 1887, I woke up and, glancing through the rails of my cot, saw my eldest sister, Toni, twelve years my senior, crying and fixing something on her hat – perhaps a black veil. 'What's the matter?' I asked. She cried even more than before and replied: 'Go on sleeping. You will know soon enough, poor child.' Without more ado I lay down and went back to sleep. I knew her even then to be somewhat exalted and did not take her too seriously. Later I heard my brother Max crying. He was my pal, only four years older than myself. He used abusive language towards our family doctor, whom I did not like either, since he smelled of carbolic acid and his ear, which he insisted on putting against my bare back, was always cold and tickled. But Max said he was the murderer of our mother. She died of what is now known as appendicitis, but in those days they called it peritonitis and did not know that a quick surgical operation could have saved her life.

I was permitted to enter the death room, where I saw something folded in white linen. The shape of 'it' reminded me of the chandelier in our living room when it was wrapped in linen for the summer. I was quite unaware of the gruesome reality. They spoke about the funeral and whether or not I should be taken along. It was finally decided that I was not to attend, and I was left at home with a new toy, something to shoot through a hole with a rubber spring. All this and more I recall perfectly well. But there was then no grief nor fear nor any sense of loss. My later life alone shows that I never stopped longing for my mother and that for the deeper layers of my ego she was not dead.

A few weeks after my mother's death we children gathered in the living room, and my sister Toni played cheerful tunes on the piano. My brother Max, a comedian by nature, performed some eccentric dance and I sang. All of a sudden my sister – I said before that she easily became hysterical – stopped playing, rose to her feet, and, pointing at one corner of the room, exclaimed: 'See, see, there!' I looked in the given direction and saw – nothing. I asked: 'What is there?' She answered: 'Mother's ghost!' I looked again, but there was definitely nothing of the kind to be seen. Toni began to sob and mumbled: 'She threatened me with her finger. I should not have played the piano, oh, I shouldn't have done it!'

I was quite disappointed. They had read me fairy tales, and I was already familiar with the idea of a ghost and would have liked to see one. But I never did, neither then nor at any other time in my life, and by now I have given up all hope. In the 1920s, with occult waves running high in Vienna, there was a famous medium named Rudi Schneider, a few of whose meetings I attended. Whenever I came, however, either nothing happened at all or the things which did happen were obvious frauds. It was terribly boring. Some twenty years after the event I asked my sister what, if anything, she had seen in that corner, where a pale plaster cast of Plato had stood on its greenish column. She did not remember the incident at all. Is it not a strange world in which we live! She saw a ghost and does not remember, while I remember everything but did not see it.

When I turned seven I became a voracious reader of fairy tales. The *Arabian Nights* and Hans Christian Andersen built a second world for me, and the so-called real world did not always seem to me to be the real one. Andersen's animism, which made household objects talk and walk and argue among themselves, just suited me and my childish philosophy. The flat-iron travelling over the board and therefore presuming, silly thing, that it was a locomotive, the paper scissors imagining themselves a dancer because of their two long legs, the kitchen pot disparaging the cucumber as an 'ordinary kitchen vegetable', were all delightful, gay, vivid companions to my fancy. Among them I found welcome confirmation of my animistic thinking, so much happier than the dry realities or abstractions of so-called real life.

The tales of the *Arabian Nights* filled me with pessimism, but a delightful pessimism, because of the invariably happy ending. From an unsealed bottle a dreadful ghost smoked skywards, ready to strangle the innocent fisherman. A merchant, spitting out a date stone, unwittingly killed an invisible ghost and his wrathful father sprang into being. Aladdin, greatest of all street Arabs, was lured into a subterranean cave and there, freezing and in darkness, doomed to death by starvation. Such was life – cruel, unjust, unfeeling. I sometimes felt all alone, one helpless child against all those stronger, self-satisfied, powerful adults.

There were dangers everywhere, for example the two brothers who were about twelve when I was eight. Every day I had to cross their path on my way to school. They lay in ambush and struck me over the head with their rulers. They were bigger than I, more aggressive, and, what is more, they were organized. Police, law, justice exist only for adults, while boys still live like Indians on the warpath. Adults remain all too often unaware of this and think that a child's life is full of joy. For a while I helped myself with the ruse of telling the two brothers that I had the high school boys on my side, and they believed this and left me alone. But when, after a time, no high school boys showed up, they took their revenge on me and pelted me with snowballs. But what snowballs! They broke enormous blocks from the heaps shovelled up at the kerb and almost buried me under the avalanche. There was really no sense in fighting back; I had to run away. My aunt came down the street, and I rushed to her, looking for salvation behind her rather wide and rotund form. But what did I have to hear from her? 'You coward!' she cried, 'Don't run away! Why don't you fight like a man?' There you could see what an adult knows of a boy's life. What is the use of fighting when two giants are pitted against one featherweight!

Something had to be done about these and other equally hostile events. I looked in the books and reread some of the Arabian stories, the adventures of Sindbad, the strange things which occurred to Prince Shemsuddin, and whatever else the 'expurgated' edition for childen yielded. I sat on the windowsill and thought deeply until I finally came up with a solution. It seemed as though everything around me was unreal, a sort of gigantic fraud put up in order to fool me. All that pretended to be real and respectable was but a feint; men at home, on the street, in school, were phantoms playing the parts of human beings in order to deceive me. There was but one reality: I, myself. I came from somewhere, had been kidnapped perhaps, and set down, for reasons not known to me, in a world of struggle, forced to live in the midst of an inimical lot. How to fathom the unfathomable? At times I felt paralysed. At other times I was encouraged to investigate the mystery. I then began to run, stopped abruptly, and quickly turned round with the idea that the magicians, not expecting my surprising manoeuvre, would be caught unawares and would reveal to me their true shapes. I also stared at people in order to ascertain their real nature. I did not get very far with my methods. I could, however, create an intermediary layer between myself, the only absolute reality, and the inimical outer world. This interposed layer was not quite as real as myself, to be sure, but it belonged to me just the same.

My infantile philosophy was a forerunner of my later psychoanalytic insight. Things were not what they seemed. It was hard, almost impossible, to explore what they actually were. There was my sister Toni pretending that she saw ghosts. I did not believe it, indeed I had reason to distrust her. There was, for example, that big garden party to celebrate her birthday. She did not come down to greet her guests, but suffered a migraine attack and lay in her darkened room with a wet towel around her head. Her beau, Emil, had failed to come. It grew late and he had been quite given up when at last he rang the bell. Like the heroine of an old-fashioned play, Toni sailed into the room, her white masquerade like a crown around her brow, exclaiming, 'Oh, Emil is here! Now I am happy again!' I did not like this stuff and wasted not a moment's thought on it. It did not form part of my own great problem of the unfathomable. Children with their incorruptible sense of reality can see through all kinds of make-believe. Toni, I knew, was a make-believer. I offer this insignificant contribution as the oldest foundation of my early and eager understanding of Freud's work. From childhood onwards I was prepared for this mighty light in the dark caves of tenebrous mysticism. I presume that Freud, too, had to pass through similar recesses in his early years, but we will probably never learn what his earliest

experiences were. I remember my own struggles too well to
doubt for a moment that the adolescent Freud, who, in his own
words, wanted 'to understand some of the puzzles of this
world', felt the same need to bridge the cleft between what we
know and what, before Freud, only mystics and metaphysicians
pretended to know.

★

My own early experiences included Frau Schreiber, my nurse.[3]
My pen almost refuses to call Frau Schreiber a nurse, for a nurse
nowadays is a superior being – a lady in white shoes, young,
beautiful or, if not that, then stern and awe-inspiring. Frau
Schreiber's boots were black with elastic sides which had lost
their elasticity before I was born. They were doing service then,
when she came to our home, and she was still wearing them
when she left, when I was seven. She is my earliest
reminiscence, almost legendary, like the time of the Nibelungs,
who came down the Danube some thousand years ago. In a play
by Johann Nestroy there is repartee between a porter and
an elderly lady which fits Frau Schreiber perfectly: *She*: 'I, too,
was young once . . .' *He*: 'That I can imagine.' *She*: '. . .
and attractive.' *He*: 'That I can't imagine!'[4] Speaking of
the Nibelungs: my parents, who were full of the Wagnerian
enthusiasm of those days, named me Siegfried. I was always
ashamed of that name, which was too glorious to be used on
weekdays, so they called me Fritz, while on my birth certificate I
was Siegfried until the American government permitted me to
put an end to that ignominy, when I got my citizenship papers.

Frau Schreiber had mysterious qualities: some good, some
bad. She kept a bottle of Slivovitz hidden behind the porcelain
stove and about once a week the old lady tanked up. She was
forty-five, or at least this was the never-changing age she
admitted to throughout the time we knew her. We were a
dramatic family, given to histrionics, and she belonged to the
family. She would shove aside the table standing in the middle
of the nursery, pose herself there solidly and pointing her right
hand to the ceiling exclaim: 'Not a day longer will I stay in this
house!' She looked like Medea or some other tragic heroine, and
though the gesture was quite impressive, even I began to feel
that there was not much substance behind her threat.

Among Frau Schreiber's heroic activities were her trips to the
dentist around the corner. She had her few remaining teeth torn
out of her jaws and replaced by a false set mounted on livid red

gums, which I saw every morning in a glass of water on her night table. This may sound disgusting, and perhaps I should dwell more on the higher nature of man. But since I am recalling personal experiences, I must say that one of the most horrendous was the dark waiting room at the dentist's, and the red water glass the dentist gave her to rinse her mouth with, which struck me as being full of blood. The world was indeed full of inexplicable things. Nothing could have induced me to go to a man in white, open my mouth voluntarily and allow him to yank out my teeth. She did it and even paid for it. As for the disgusting side, in retrospect there was nothing really disgusting in those sweet old days. What Hamlet says about good and evil applies to disgust too. Nothing in itself is truly disgusting. How we think about things furnishes these descriptive adjectives. On the other hand, the cereal served up to me almost every day was disgusting, believe me. To get this titbit into me Frau Schreiber invented a trick, or perhaps the trick existed before and she only employed it. There was the cereal spread all over a plate as white and enormous as an arctic landscape. She criss-crossed it with the spoon, the squares representing all the familiar streets of our neighbourhood – Schottenring, Gonzagagaße, Franz Josefs Kai, Rudolfsplatz – until I'd eaten the whole map. Sometimes she ran out of streets, and under protest I had to eat one square for Mama, one for Papa, one for each of my brothers, one for sister, for my aunts and uncles, and even for Mila, the Czech cook, if necessary.

As Frau Schreiber made me see it, the comprehensible centre of the universe was the grocer on the corner. There was a way up from the grocer which led to a delicatessen, three blocks away. There was also a way down to the smaller grocer with a narrow entrance to a dark, overstuffed shop, where everything you bought savoured of kerosene. Still, he was a little cheaper than the real grocer and a lot cheaper than the almost unattainable delicatessen. My parents were rarely at home for dinner, so Frau Schreiber and I had to go out to buy our dinner. The small grocer sold no ham at all. The ordinary grocer's ham was maroon coloured and very salty. The ham at the delicatessen was pink and fragrant. I was given to understand that this was beyond any normal man's reach. The same was true of the frankfurters or whatever else may have formed the backbone of a regular dinner for Frau Schreiber and me.

My sister Toni, who was the eldest of the children, studied drama at the Conservatorium. Frau Schreiber and I had to call

1. Saint Stephen's Cathedral, symbol of old Vienna (from an eighteenth-century print).

for Toni several times a week at her school at the other side of the inner city. Frau Schreiber knew all the short-cuts. We regularly passed Saint Stephen's, the Gothic cathedral, which was the natural centre of our crossings, partly because Frau Schreiber refreshed her soul, at least the sober part of it, by dipping her fingertips into the holy water font at the entrance, followed by a hasty genuflexion on passing the altar. As far as I can remember we were always in a hurry, although I don't know why. Saint Stephen's Cathedral is a landmark. Dozens of songs attest to the beauty of its gigantic spire, and the Viennese consider the tower as everlasting – as much a part of the city as the Danube and the vineyards on the hills. It is about six hundred years old and has seen much exciting history. Yet this marvellous edifice is a stranger in the city: the savage scream to a medieval God which the minster expresses is not understood.

2. The Burgtheater on the newly designed Vienna Ringstraße, late nineteenth-century.

The easygoing, singing, wine-drinking, laughingly sophisticated Viennese show their lack of understanding by calling the spire 'Steffl', the diminutive of Stephen.

Frau Schreiber's penny-pinching may give the impression that my parents were poor, but this was not the case. My father was a broker on the Vienna stock exchange, and although his position could not be compared with that of a New York broker, he had considerable money to spend and gave his children, who finally numbered seven, a good education.[5] Particularly for his first born, my sister, who was generally considered a genius, no expense was spared. She had an English teacher and a French teacher, she took lessons in fencing, practised roller skating at an indoor club, and even became a pupil of the celebrated Fritz Krastel, male lead in the Burgtheater, who was adored by débutantes, matrons and aristocrats as old as the hills. He took my sister on without charge because he thought so highly of her and also of my father, who was a match for him when wine and champagne were imbibed. Later, his affectation took on such proportions that he could hardly be endured on the stage. However, in the taverns he remained a hero to the end, which this very heroism helped to bring on. I saw very little of him on the stage, because in the eighties I wasn't taken to the theatre and in the late nineties he had already become a wreck. Yet I remember well

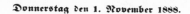
Donnerstag den 1. November 1888.

14. Vorstellung im neuen Abonnement.

Die Ahnfrau.

Trauerspiel in fünf Aufzügen von Grillparzer.

Graf Zdenko von Borotin	—	—	—	Hr. Lewinsky.
Bertha, seine Tochter	—	—	—	Frl. Barsescu.
Jaromir	—	—	—	Hr. Krastel.
Boleslav	—	—	—	Hr. Kracher.
Günther, Castellan	—	—	—	Hr. Arnau.
Ein Hauptmann	—	—	—	Hr. Schreiner.
Ein Soldat	—	—	—	Hr. Gabillon.
Die Ahnfrau des Hauses Borotin	—	—	—	Fr. Bauer.

Soldaten und Diener.

Die Dekorationen ausgeführt vom Dekorationsmaler Herrn Gilbert Lehner.

Zwischen dem 2. und 3. Akt 20 Minuten Pause.

Der freie Eintritt (mit Ausnahme der Hof-Freibillets) ist heute nicht gestattet.

Unpäßlich: Frau Wolter. Fr. Mitterwurzer. Hr. Baumeister.

Freitag	2. Die Ahnfrau.		Montag	5. Die Journalisten.
Samstag	3. König und Bauer.		Dinstag	6. Die Journalisten.
Sonntag	4. König und Bauer.			

Preise der Plätze:

Eine Loge im Parterre 1. und 2. Rang	fl. 25.—	Ein Sitz auf der 3. Galerie 2. bis 4. Reihe	fl. 2.—
Eine Loge im 3. Stock	fl. 12.—	Ein Sitz auf der 3. Galerie 5 bis 7. Reihe	fl. 1.—
Ein Sitz im Parquet 1. Reihe	fl. 5.—	Ein Sitz auf der 4. Galerie 1. Reihe.	fl. 1.50
Ein Sitz im Parquet 2. bis 4. Reihe	fl. 4.—	Ein Sitz auf der 4. Galerie 2. bis 6. Reihe	fl. 1.—
Ein Sitz im Parquet 5. bis 9. Reihe	fl. 3.50	Ein Sitz auf der 4. Galerie 7. bis 9. Reihe	fl. —.70
Ein Sitz im Parquet 10. bis 13. Reihe	fl. 3.—	Eintritt in das Stehparterre (nur Herren	
Ein Sitz im Parterre 1. Reihe	fl. 3.—	gestattet)	fl. 1.—
Ein Sitz im Parterre 2. bis 5. Reihe	fl. 2.50	Eintritt in die 4. Galerie (Stehplatz)	fl. —.40
Ein Sitz auf der 3. Galerie 1. Reihe	fl. 2.50		

Zu jeder im Repertoire angekündigten Vorstellung erfolgt **Tags vorher** bis 1 Uhr Nachmittags die Ausgabe der Stammsitze, von 1 bis 5 Uhr Nachmittags der allgemeine Vorverkauf der restirenden Sitze gegen Entrichtung der Vorkaufsgebühr.

Diese beträgt für einen Parquetsitz erste Reihe fl. 1, für Parquet- und Parterresitze 50 kr., für Galeriesitze 30 kr. Die Vorkaufsgebühr wird für Parquetsitze auch noch am Tage der Vorstellung **bis 12 Uhr Mittags**, für die anderen Plätze nur bis zum Tage vorher eingehoben. Im Falle einer Abänderung am Tage gelten für alle Sitzkategorien die gewöhnlichen Tagespreise.

Kassa-Eröffnung 6 Uhr. Anfang 7 Uhr. Ende vor 10 Uhr.

3. Playbill for the performance of Grillparzer's *Die Ahnfrau* (*The Ancestress*) at the Burgtheater, attended by the eight-year-old Wittels with Frau Schreiber on All Saints' Day 1888.

how the great man who, like almost all the leading actors then, was six feet tall, danced me on his shoe and dandled me on his knee.

The K. K. Hofburgtheater, which being translated means Imperial Royal Court Castle Theatre – what an institution it was! The Burgtheater was much better than anything Germany ever produced. They celebrated the German language, glorified Shakespeare and the German classics, but included French

comedies as well, within the limits of what young countesses
were permitted to see. Most of the actors were engaged for life,
and they were recognized and beloved when they walked
through the streets of Vienna. Their mannerisms were imitated,
and it was easy to emulate them as they all had their
idiosyncrasies, this being perhaps a quality common to all
important figures. There was the heroic gesture and tragic
scream of Charlotte Wolter; the elegance of Adolf von Sonnental
with his perpetually stuffed nose; Josef Lewinsky, not the prize-
fighter from Chicago but the demoniacal intriguer who played
Mephistopheles, roaring like a tiger, lion or jaguar; and then, of
course, Krastel himself, whose shoulders always heaved when he
declaimed. And did he declaim! On 1 November, All Saints'
Day, all Vienna rushed to the cemeteries, and the theatres played
ghost tragedies. At the Burgtheater it was always *The Ancestress*
by Nestroy's counterpart in tragedy, Franz Grillparzer. He died
in 1871, and I could tell tales without end about this typically
crabby Viennese playwright. Every child in Vienna has heard of
him, yet he is unknown outside the city's ramparts. *The
Ancestress* was not his best, but it was his most popular tragedy,
and Krastel played the leading role, the noble brigand Jaromir.[6]

In a castle haunted by the ghost of the Ancestress (played by
Wolter) lives Count Borodin with his lovely daughter Bertha.
One morning when Bertha is out riding, she is kidnapped by
robbers, but a brave youth named Jaromir, whom Bertha does
not know, rescues her and brings her safely home, not,
however, without the couple first falling desperately in love. She
tells her father of her love, and he is favourably inclined to their
marriage. But, in the natural progress of occurrences (as Nestroy
would say), they first suspect, then are almost certain and finally
learn the awful truth that Jaromir is the captain of the gang of
robbers.[7] How admirably Mr Krastel spoke these lines:

> Yes, 'tis I, you wretched woman,
> Yes, 'tis I, whom you have named.
> I'm the bailiff's prey and hunted
> I'm the people's cursed, shunted
> I'm the robber Jaromir![8]

Bertha faints, but the worst is yet to come. It is disclosed that
Jaromir is the old Count's son, who was kidnapped in early
childhood and reared by thieves. The Ancestress enters and
leaves a dagger. Jaromir, innocent of the knowledge that the

Count is his father, kills old Borodin with the bewitched family weapon. I no longer remember whether Bertha learns that her lover, the murderer of her father, is also her brother, but I wouldn't be at all surprised if she does. Anyway, she stabs herself to death with the same dagger. Jaromir hides in the cellar – or shall we say crypt – where the Ancestress, who resembles Bertha like two peas in a pod, appears. The Ancestress, whom he believes to be his beloved Bertha, reveals to him his accursed descent. Nothing loath, he still wants to embrace her, whereupon he drops dead. Thus the entire family is wiped out, and the Ancestress is at last laid to eternal rest.

> Open up, oh quiet dome
> Let the Ancestress go home.[9]

Perhaps I should have chosen a better example for the glory of the Burgtheater. But *The Ancestress* happens to be the first and for a long time the only play I saw. Mr Krastel gave us tickets and we went, Frau Schreiber and I. Today one would not allow a seven-year-old boy to see such a nightmare, but there were no psychoanalysts in those days to prevent it. I am not sure whether or not it disturbed my sleep. I do remember, though, that we had to hurry home because it was so late.

No doubt some readers will wonder why I do not speak more of my mother. But she died when I was six years old, and all I remember about her is that she was a beautiful woman and that she died. Frau Schreiber was the recipient of some of my uprooted and freely floating attachment. But if I'm not mistaken, most of this kind of love embraced my city and a few villages and towns in the city's environs. Looking back, I see myself strolling through the oldest streets and buildings with a never-ending longing for something which had gone.

★

The house in which I was born in the early 1880s was number 10, Nestroystraße. This address is of special significance, even though my parents moved downtown only two years later. Johann Nestroy, almost unknown outside that city, is the incarnation of the spirit of Vienna, just as Rabelais symbolizes the French or Mark Twain the American spirit. Nestroy's satire, enveloped in the petty-bourgeois tongue of the early Victorian era – he died in 1862 – is so typically Viennese that one cannot be really Viennese without being a good deal Nestroyan as well. He

4 and 5. The Actor-dramatist Johann Nestroy in characteristic roles from his own plays: (*above*) the poet Leicht in *Weder Lorbeerbaum noch Bettelstab* and the soldier Sansquartier in *Zwölf Mädchen in Uniform* and (*facing page*) the heroine Judith (actually Joab in disguise) in *Judith und Holofernes*.

was a tall, gaunt fellow with a Voltairean nose, who played many parts in the comedies he wrote. The world would have known and admired him had he lived in London or Paris. But in our coffee-houses we knew how great we Viennese were, greater even than the geniuses and recognized talents with which western cities abounded, while we remained unsung, ignored by the world abroad.

Judith und Holofernes
Hr. Scholz Nestroy und Frau Schmitt. 3 1849

Instead of relating the difficulties which accompanied my weaning period, I'd better say a little more about the man on whose street I was born. He once said, 'I have the deepest contempt for all people, including myself, and I seldom err.'[10] To me this aphorism is of a depth to be fathomed only by great philosophers. Its cynicism, coupled with a disarming candour and phrased in his irresistible manner, is a product of Vienna, the city in which I lived for almost fifty years and which now lives in me. When I and others like me are gone the Vienna we loved will be gone for ever.

From the beginning of the nineteenth century Vienna was an admixture of Catholicism, a centralized monarchy, and the ideals of the French revolution which infiltrated society against the will of both the Church and the government. These ideals were somewhat subdued, but fundamentally constituted an essential part of every intelligent individual in Vienna. Napoleon had not been in Schönbrunn in vain. He was there twice, in 1805 and in 1809, and when he left, the principles of liberty and equality remained like shells after a receding tide. Prince Metternich,

Austria's Chancellor until 1848, snuffed out every spark of liberty with what was then considered brutal force. He was an aristocrat and moreover Viennese and therefore had to yield somewhat to the force of wit. Nestroy was often arrested for his political jokes, but the jailers themselves sat in the stalls and applauded. His subjects were often the plight of the little man, the arrogance of the *nouveau riche*, and stupidity in general. His philosophical butlers, porters and boot-blacks hissed his revolutionary truth into the audience, usually adorned in the peculiarly convoluted metaphors of bygone days. The hypocritically humble butler says to his employer, who has recently experienced some trivial contretemps, 'The idea of fate trifling with a millionaire like you!' Or, 'A million dollars is an excellent rampart from which you can look down pleasantly on the battalions of fate marching by.'[11] When I quote Nestroy's sayings to non-Viennese, I would like to explain their philosophical connotations and their contempt of man. I refrain from doing so because it would be counter-Nestroyan. 'Leave 'em alone,' he would say. 'Supposing they don't understand?'

In 1848 we had a revolution. There were revolutionary flames all over Europe, and a spark flew to Vienna, forcing Metternich the oppressor to resign. A citizen guard was organized: even Nestroy was drafted, and he stood as a guard on the south side of the Ferdinandsbrücke, rifle in hand, sardonic smile on his face. In his immediate neighbourhood were his theatre, where he had for many years made all Vienna laugh, and the coffee-house where he played cards daily before the performance. It was then – in those days of revolutionary enthusiasm – that he formulated his celebrated definition of progress: 'Progress has the peculiar nature of being always only half as big as it looks.'[12] A few months later the revolution was suppressed, its leaders shot and some Hungarian generals hanged. The new freedom of the press hadn't lasted very long, and the censor returned. 'A censor,' Nestroy exclaimed, 'is a man transformed into a pencil, or vice versa, who bites off authors' heads as they swim in the current of their inspiration.'[13] It is difficult to translate Nestroy. The fragrance of his Viennese idiom is lost. What perhaps can be conveyed are the ambivalent tendencies, his combination of sublime ideas with trivialities, pessimism and optimism, love and hate. This marriage of incompatible emotions became an Austrian speciality. The French say: that which is not clear is not French. The Viennese might say of themselves: those who are not ambivalent are not Viennese.

The world holds to the opinion, for various reasons, that people from Vienna talk a great deal, whereas just the opposite is true. Viennese can sit together, with or without wine, for hours without opening their mouths. They are sharp in criticism and strong in approval, but they prefer not to express either. This is important, otherwise one would take them for dull. A few years ago in Vienna I listened to an excited debate (if you can call it that) carried on almost entirely alone by a Hungarian painter in a group. Nobody contradicted him. He was arguing that critics who do not themselves paint have no right to talk about painting. He said that it was as though a fish would judge a bird in the air. He chose this metaphor because the famous zoologist Bernhard Hatshek was among us. Hatshek sat there as silently as the rest of us. Finally the exasperated Hungarian harangued him personally: 'Am I right, Professor?' To which Hatshek quietly answered 'No.' And that was all he said and all that there was to it.

I must tell you more about Nestroy and his time, which had changed only slightly when my time came. One of his most effective mediums was parody. Parody, vitriolic, sarcastic, often anonymous, always reflects a civilization which makes people homogeneous. To appreciate the parody, one must be sufficiently interested in the original: a tragedy, an opera, a poem, or whatever it is. Most famous among Nestroy's parodies was his *Judith and Holofernes*, which even now is still remembered in Vienna, while his *Tannhäuser* parody has faded against Wagner's glorious genius. Friedrich Hebbel, the German author, had had his tragedy *Judith* produced in a Viennese theatre. Holofernes is depicted as a superman whose equal does not exist on earth. Judith has to seduce him and then cut off his head. She is in the throes of a dilemma when she can't make up her mind whether she is in love with the great man or not, and later, towards the end of the play, she anticipates the natural consequences of her seduction and wonders what she will tell her child. Here was a subject replete with possibilities for travesty, and Nestroy lost no time. He showed up the shallow vanity of the superman by making him say: 'I am terrific. If I could only wrestle with myself and find out who is stronger, I or me.' In Hebbel's play Holofernes kills several men successively on the very slightest of provocations. The parody retains this display of heroism but adds an anticlimax: after the deed the hero cries out, 'Take them away, I won't have my house cluttered up!' Later the Jewish army arrives. 'Eyes right!' shouts the sergeant. Private Ike asks: 'Why? Is there anything to see there?' Another private grumbles: 'What right has he to order us about? One Jew's as good as another.' Toward the end, one of Holofernes's Assyrians shouts: 'The general has lost his head!'[14] At which all of them flee. After Nestroy's parody no one could watch Hebbel's five-act tragedy without giggling, for he had killed a noble work of genius with his barbed cynicism. As I have already said, a bit of Nestroy's spirit is to be found in every Viennese: it isn't easy to fool him, but at the same time it's very easy, given his ambivalent nature. The question of whether the spirit of Vienna will succumb to Prussianism is identical with the question as to whether this city will remain Nestroyan.

★

After this somewhat prolonged digression – I'm afraid this book may consist of nothing but digressions – I'll return to my own diapers. When I was two years old, as I have said, we moved to the centre of the city. There was a friendly courtyard outside which I could see from my window, and an old brick wall, half denuded of its plaster, which reminded me of a map. Later I enlarged the idea of the friendly courtyard to include the entire neighbourhood in which we lived, the city centre which is the oldest part of Vienna. The buildings were grey with age and impressed me so deeply that the history of Vienna became my first hobby. I grew up in the oldest part of Vienna, where the ancient Romans had erected their settlement some two thousand years before, allegedly under the name of Vindabona. No one knows exactly what the name signifies. Some believe that the modern name of Vienna derives from the first syllable and that the word meant the city of good winds, a gentler forerunner of Chicago. Others give a different etymology, for instance that a Slav tribe lived there. The name 'Windish' still prevails among some Slavs. I would rather not argue with etymologists. My good old friend Josef Popper used to say: 'I can see how things are now, but how they were long ago, I can't see.'[15]

The fact that we lived among buildings which were grey and heavy with antiquity made an impression on me which does not fade, even when compared with the vista from my Central Park West apartment.[16] In my time it became a rather dirty business district, and when I say dirty I do not only mean this literally. I saw beyond all those offices with their imposing signs advertising firms of questionable solidity, their green lampshades and the trucks on the streets loaded with big bales of textiles. I saw the city as it had looked long before my time, or rather a number of cities throughout the centuries. In its long history Vienna was destroyed again and again, only to be resurrected from the ashes. The Roman castle disappeared from the surface of the earth and several hundred years later we see a fishing village in its stead with a little church on a hill overlooking a sandy riverbank, where, besides the fishing barges, broad boats landed bringing salt from the mines up the river, destined for Constantinople, the Orient and points further east. Next we see the wild Hungarians coming from the east astride their small Mongolian horses, killing the fishermen, raping their wives, stealing their children and burning the wooden church, because they were pagans like their relatives, the Huns. The church can still be seen from the top of three flights of steps, and the village around it was built anew over and over again, and finally the Hungarians became Christians themselves, settling as peasants in the plains of the lower Danube.

Later the village again disappeared, not destroyed by flame and sword, but overgrown by a stately city where the commodities of the Orient were exchanged for the goods of the west and the people would have amassed fortunes, had not the princes, first of the glorious house of Babenberg and later of the even more glorious house of Habsburg, taken most of the profits. Churches, monasteries and convents sprouted like mushrooms, and what the princes left went into the pockets of the clergy and those of the Jews as well, although the Jews were robbed, killed, expelled from time to time, while the clergy established itself for good and collected gold in the name of the Lord whom the Jews had crucified. It was a colourful world. The crusaders, full of their divine mission, passed through the city and would have been impartial and taken the money from the monasteries as well, had they not been told that it was much more ethical to take it from the Jews.

The Jews were expelled from Vienna *en masse* several times. Christians were not allowed to take interest on money loans; Jews, on the other hand, were not permitted to trade. So they became the money-lenders and thus accumulated gold. They became more hated for usury than for the killing of the Lord, although not by the princes. The populace repeatedly asked their princes, not only in medieval Vienna, to expel the Jews, but the princes needed them to raise revenue for their royal households and expensive wars. The Jews, who were forced to live in ghettoes like concentration camps, could always be squeezed when the princes wanted money. So the unfortunate race was

6. Monument on the Judenplatz in Vienna, designed to suggest that the massacre of the Jews in 1421 was caused by their refusal to accept Christian baptism.

protected by the various monarchs until their people's demands became so urgent that they had to give in and sign the order of expulsion. But the problem remained: how to wage wars with no money? So, after thirty, fifty or a hundred years, the Jews were re-established and the cycle began anew.

The year 1421 was particularly joyful for the Christians in Vienna because all the Jews were driven to a place outside the ramparts and burnt at an enormous stake. At that time a Habsburg prince, Albrecht V, lived in the city, and as the Habsburgs were always especially devoted to religion, the motive behind the burning of these devil's roasts was undoubtedly the glory of God. The people of his day had the same reason for their antagonism towards Jews as they have now: they felt exploited by the money-lenders. So the king took away all the Jews' possessions and kept them for himself, because he could no longer bear to see his beloved people exploited. This gruesome massacre of the Jews on the village green north of the River Wien is still commemorated by a Gothic inscription on the wall of a hoary building on the Judenplatz in Vienna.[17]

The plague visited Vienna several times. Each time half the city's population was wiped out, and always popular prejudice held the Jews responsible. It was widely believed that they had poisoned the wells, killed Christian children and used their blood for cannibalistic orgies at Easter. Add to this their strange predilection for stealing the sacred Host from the altars of the churches and polluting it in the vilest way, and who could doubt that these people were capable of crucifying the Lord? What was incomprehensible, however, was that Jesus himself was a Jew, who could not deny that he had the blood of at least one Jewish grandparent in his ancestry – and probably four![18]

I am also tempted to describe the two Turkish sieges and how the Turks looted and destroyed all but the fortified inner circle of Vienna; also the exploits of that noble knight, Prince Eugene of Savoy; and more important still, all the Viennese musicians from Mozart to Strauss. But since I promised memoirs, I shall cut short the history of Vienna, a hobby which the reader probably does not share with me, and return to my personal experiences, humble as they are compared with all these great kings and knights in shining armour.[19]

2

Freud and the Vienna Medical School

I graduated from the University of Vienna in 1904, and from then on I was a doctor. To this day I have not ceased wondering at this fact, because I am and always have been given to the humanities. However, the atmosphere of the Vienna medical school was such that you could not become too bad a physician. It would really have required superhuman resistance to the spirit of the place to have failed to imbibe the essence of medical wisdom offered, even forced upon us by teachers who, although no longer quite as great as the giants who founded the international reputation of the Vienna school, still lived in the unbroken traditions of their work.

Here we see another side of the Vienna, not the gay city with her lovely women and cavaliers, but the scientific side with its imperturbable analysis of phenomena. I do not consider it my business to give a detailed picture of the medical school. Others have done so, and many doctors in America have reason to remember the General Hospital in Vienna of the year 1900 and later. Do they recall the old gynaecologist Chrobak, obstetrician of the Imperial Court, who had a big sign in his auditorium: *Primum est non nocere!* (First of all: do no harm!)? Each year the old man, cheeks pink and puffed from too many dinner parties, began his lectures by solemnly pointing to the sign and declaring, 'Gentlemen, *primum est non nocere!*' He was not among the greatest teachers but his principle was great. It was at the Gynaecological Institute in Vienna that Dr Semmelweis, long before Pasteur, found that puerperal fever was caused by doctors' carelessness in examining women in childbed. They never bothered to sterilize their instruments and their hands. This momentous discovery was glorified in Dr Chrobak's sign.

In my day there still existed at the medical school the concept of 'therapeutic nihilism'.[1] Medical science ended where therapy began, giving way to an impenetrable thicket of art, personal influence, even fraud, which the medical teachers in Vienna abhorred. This attitude towards therapy prevailed for internal diseases. Surgery was different. Here, Lord Lister's triumphant antisepsis and asepsis were fully realized. The internists exerted all their acumen and skill in the exhaustive study of diseases and lost very little time teaching therapy. As diagnosticians they were deeply scholarly. Their clinical intuition was often tantamount to an incredible lucidity. Once Professor Neusser, after citing conclusive evidence, declared a patient's condition to be hopeless: this patient was doomed and nothing could save him, not even God Almighty. Yet this very professor never mentioned therapy or, if he did, he would end his learned exposition with the words: 'to be treated accordingly'.

It may sound inhuman to the layman, but a post mortem examination was always a celebrated day of judgment. There, in the Pathological Institute, diagnoses were confirmed or rejected. When an error had occurred we gathered in our chief's private office and discussed the error so as to avoid it in the future. Science follows in unwritten cycles of thirty to fifty years. Around 1900 the thing to do in internal medicine was to find out the nature and causes of diseases. Medical science was then devoted to this almost exclusively. Later came the more advanced application of therapy. By that time Vienna's great doctors had died and those still living looked askance at the new and noisy generation of healers.

Although Freud, as the world knows, was a magnificent healer, even he, with his roots in the tradition of Vienna's medical school, never hesitated to say that it is much more important to find out how our psychic apparatus functions than to cure a certain number of wretched individuals. Freud had no quarrel with anyone who feels that this is not the correct attitude for a doctor to assume. He devoted his life to science, and healing is just a by-product of his endeavours. This point of view is diametrically opposed to the idea that science can never be an aim in itself, but that it must be useful to society. Naturally, medical science must cure. But the true spirit of science heals better than the messianic spirit, which can never be separated from mysticism. Vienna's nihilistic school has probably helped more patients than all the blaring ignoramuses who heal in the fog.

After my graduation from medical school in 1904, I lived for four more years in the General Hospital of Vienna under the

7. Fritz Wittels
as a young man.

quaint titles of hospitant, aspirant and secondary physician. I
strolled through the ten great courtyards of the enormous
building, with its five thousand beds, more or less resigned to
the fate of a regular physician. For almost a year I was assigned
to surgery, and learned there that I would never be adept at this
branch of medicine. Not that I wasn't skilful; I could handle
scalpel, needle and silk as well as the next, but my rivals in
the department were so much more eager to attack their fellow
men with armed hands that I found myself forced into the
background. I had to remain an anaesthetist and to work in the
'septic' clinic most of the time, while they performed the most
wonderful appendectomies and herniotomies and surpassed one
another in the techniques of resection. I felt more at home in

COPIA.

Q. F. F. F. Q. S.

SUMMIS AUSPICIIS AUGUSTISSIMI IMPERATORIS AC REGIS

FRANCISCI IOSEPHI I

IN UNIVERSITATE LITTERARUM VINDOBONENSI

NOS

GUSTAVUS EQUES DE ESCHERICH

PHILOSOPHIAE DOCTOR MATHEMATICIS PROFESSOR PUBLICUS ORDINARIUS IMPERATORIS AUSTRIAE
A CONSILIIS AULAE CAES. ACADEMIAE SCIENTIARUM VINDOBONENSIS SOCIUS
EQUES ORDINIS CORONAE FERREAE CL. III.

H. T. UNIVERSITATIS RECTOR

ANTONIUS WEICHSELBAUM

MEDICINAE UNIVERSAE DOCTOR ANATOMIAE PATHOLOGICAE PROFESSOR PUBLICUS ORDINARIUS
IMPERATORIS AUSTRIAE A CONSILIIS AULAE CAES. ACADEMIAE SCIENTIARUM
VINDOBONENSIS SOCIUS EQUES ORDINIS CORONAE FERREAE CL. III.

ORDINIS MEDICORUM H. T. DECANUS

Fridericus Schauta

medicinae universae doctor artis obstetriciae professor publicus

ordinarius imperatoris austriae a consiliis aulae eques

ordinis coronae ferreae cl. III.

PROMOTOR RITE CONSTITUTUS

IN

VIRUM CLARISSIMUM

Siegfriedum Wittels

Vindobonensem

POSTQUAM EXAMINIBUS LEGITIMIS CUM DOCTRINAM TUM FACULTATEM ARTIS MEDICAE PROBAVIT

DOCTORIS UNIVERSAE MEDICINAE NOMEN ET HONORES

POTESTATEMQUE ARTEM TAM MEDICAM CHIRURGICAMQUE QUAM OPHTHALMICAM ATQUE
OBSTETRICIAM EXERCENDI CONTULIMUS IN EIUSQUE REI FIDEM HASCE LITTERAS UNIVERSITATIS
SIGILLO SANCIENDAS CURAVIMUS.

VINDOBONAE, DIE XXI. M. Maii   MCMIV.

G. v. Escherich   *A. Weichselbaum m. p.*   *F. Schauta m. p.*

L. S.

8. Certificate conferring on Siegfried [Fritz] Wittels the degree of Doctor of Medicine, University of Vienna, 21 May 1904.

9. A view of the Vienna General Hospital around 1900.

internal medicine, where the chief goals were still diagnoses based on percussion and consultation. For almost two years I worked under Dr Kovacs, a remarkable diagnostician. I lived in a dark room in the ninth yard of the hospital and had a good time there. Kovacs seemed to like my work, and I hoped for a while that he would make me his first assistant. And so he would have, had I not rather suddenly changed my interest from internal medicine to psychiatry, or rather to Freud's early teachings.

The first thing I heard about Freud was that there was a man in Vienna, a *Privatdozent* of neurology, who said in earnest that when a girl dreamed of an electric light bulb she meant in reality a penis. That impressed us as crazy and was the more surprising as this *Privatdozent* had previously published good neurological papers, among them one on infantile paralysis, which later appeared in Nothnagel's handbook, and another on speech disorders, which was well thought of by experts.[2] One more – we thought – who wished to become famous the sensational way, one more gone astray through over-ambition.

Psychiatry was not then popular among physicians and, in fact, has never really achieved popularity. Medicine teaches us to observe and to differentiate from among phenomena observable directly or under the microscope. Scalpel and biochemistry are made familiar to us. Anything beyond that, introspective processes especially, produces an uneasiness in the scientifically

10 and 11.   Two of Wittels's teachers: Julius Wagner-Jauregg and Sigmund Freud.

trained medical man which he does not care to hide. Hence psychiatry has tried time and again to become 'honest' by tackling its problems with the methods of experimental pathology or, at least, those of experimental psychology. The psychiatrists could see no other way of becoming fully accepted in the circle of medical specialties and they dared not make their colleagues in the other branches of medicine see the particular necessities of psychiatry. This task should not now be too difficult, after Freud's work, if only the psychiatrist would courageously follow it up. But all psychiatry is stymied because of this strange lack of courage and this resistance to Freud's work which is difficult to surmount. Wagner-Jauregg, for many years head of the Psychiatric Institute in Vienna, was always more an experimental pathologist than a psychologist. He subsequently received the Nobel Prize for his malaria treatment of general paresis. His accomplishment in this field was experimental throughout, and medical brains could enjoy it one hundred per cent. Since Freud never was honoured with the Nobel Prize, we had the feeling that the academy in Stockholm demonstratively honoured Wagner-Jauregg as an experimentalist in psychiatry, knowing that he came from a city which was the home of the greatest psychological genius of all time. All efforts to induce this academy to honour Freud proved futile.

Before Wagner-Jauregg, the head of psychiatry in Vienna was Richard Krafft-Ebing, who died in 1902. His name was internationally famous through his *Psychopathia Sexualis* of 1886, still a classic and widely read. I often attended his lectures, less for the sake of studying psychiatry than for his most impressive presentations. From him one could learn that fools were really fools, and not at all our own kind, as psychoanalysis later so unequivocally taught. He had a flair for the theatrical. His manic female patients would enter the lecture hall barefooted and with flowers entwined in their hair: he showed Ophelia in her 'amentia', Lady Macbeth wrapped in majestic melancholy, all kinds of Napoleons, Christs and less ambitious megalomaniacs as well. Once he presented a high school teacher who had delusions that he was a Secretary of State. The little man in his blue hospital gown entered the hall, and Krafft-Ebing said to him: 'Have a seat, Your Excellency.' The 'Secretary of State' with his bristly dark head looked very much like a teacher of Latin or Greek. He replied: 'Just a minute. There is an urgent edict which has to go to print first. Does one of the gentlemen write shorthand?'

A student volunteered and the minister dictated: 'His Imperial and Royal Apostolic Majesty has ordered that his title "Imperial and Royal Apostolic Majesty" be changed to "Apostolic Imperial and Royal Majesty", since his Majesty's Apostolic Majesty, deriving from the apostles, is older than his Majesty's Imperial and Royal Majesty. Signed: Apostolic Emperor and King.' The sense of order of a pedantic teacher was preserved in the midst of lunacy: he was right. Krafft-Ebing cross-examined him:

'So, you are a Secretary of State?'

'Yes, *Herr Hofrat*.'

'That means that you are my superior.'

'No, *Herr Hofrat*. You are always higher in this place than anyone else.'

'How can that be? Both of us are in civil service. I, a professor in the sixth class and you, a Secretary of State in the second.'

'That is correct,' the school teacher answered without hesitation. 'But you have to carry out a kind of supervision; hence you are my superior.'

'Don't you remember that you were in a similar condition once before when they sent you to our station?'

The patient remembered.

'We saved you then,' Krafft-Ebing continued, 'from a lot of trouble and we are doing the same for you now by preventing you from making a fool of yourself.'

The patient said: 'I know that and I feel grateful to you for it in every respect.'

'But then you should realize that you are not actually a Secretary of State but a schoolteacher.'

'You say that, *Herr Hofrat*, because you have not been correctly informed about these things.'

In this way the conversation continued for some time. It was quite entertaining and sometimes, when Krafft-Ebing was deeply involved in a patient's delusion, one was not quite sure where the joke ended. One could learn a lot from him. His was an artistic understanding coupled with a good heart. Once he demonstrated a man with melancholia accusing himself of having poisoned a hundred thousand people. Krafft-Ebing complied for a while with the man's delusions but finally said: 'Go with God, you are no more guilty than I or anybody else.' I remember another case, a manic girl who sang and danced around the professor until she finally pulled out his gold watch by the chain. With a sudden expletive Krafft-Ebing terminated the interview.

Towards the end of the nineteenth century Emil Kraepelin, who moved to Munich in 1903, instilled a new life into psychiatry. He tried with some success to describe mental diseases in a new and systematic way. In spite of this progress nobody could imagine before Freud, followed by Bleuler and Jung, that there could be sense in this nonsense. The fact that psychosis too had a meaning was also unknown ('Though this be madness, yet there is method in it'). A few years after Krafft-Ebing's death, when I was second assistant physician at the Psychiatric Institute, Kraepelin's ideas were frozen into a scheme. Our leading assistant physician simplified his work by classifying the cases in numbers from one to twenty. He rushed as quickly as possible from bed to bed in order to write his numbers on the headboards. His pince-nez hung loosely on his hard-boned nose as he looked with slight annoyance at his poor patients: it was always the same thing and not worth wasting time. He questioned them quizzically regarding the multiplication tables, the year, month and time of the day and sometimes he made them enumerate the tributaries of the Danube. When they did not know the answers, an evil smile crossed his features and he curtly said: 'No! Try once more!'

When they failed their second guess, he wrote a 9 or a 14, as the case was, on the headboard with his chalk and proceeded to the next bed. He was in a hurry because the cases had come to us for 'observation' only and were to be transferred to different state institutes as fast as possible. Only the drunkards were kept for a few days, and after their recovery from stark lunacy they were sent back to their bottles.

I no longer know what made me read Freud's first publication on psychoanalysis. His *Studies on Hysteria*, published in 1895 together with Joseph Breuer, had met with great interest. But this happened before my time. Around 1900 one did not hear much about the 'cathartic method' of 1895 in Vienna, probably because it was known that Joseph Breuer had severed his scientific relations with Freud and also because Freud, in a kind of incubation or latency period, let a few years pass without continuing the path started in the *Studies*. I read the books published by him after 1900 and was most definitely impressed. Something was no doubt now awakened in me which had slumbered from early childhood on. It was exciting indeed: I felt right away that here a discovery of enormous importance was in the making. The dream interpreters, Joseph and Daniel, were transported into scientific life, the 'other world' was illuminated, the hobgoblins of 'Fehlleistungen' (so-called Feudian slips) were discovered. One could exclaim: 'The spirits wake up, it is a pleasure to live', as the German knight Ulrich von Hutten did in the early Renaissance.[3] I knew enough of the spirit of our old medical school to anticipate a cheerful struggle with the dull brains there and I prepared myself for this struggle.

It was clear that there was more sex in the new doctrine than was palatable to the General Hospital. To me, there was another aspect of psychoanalysis which appeared startlingly significant. I was strongly impressed by the importance of repressed sexual appetites, and above all, by the concept of the unconscious displacement of affects from their point of origin, where they belong, to other ideas and tendencies, where they do not really belong, and the creation, by such displacement, of neurotics. The mechanism was vaguely known before, but no one, before Freud, was aware of the frequency and importance of the displacement of affects nor of its striking manifestations in groups as well as in individuals.

For almost a year I studied Freud's books and papers without realizing that I was living in the very building where he lectured every Saturday evening from seven to nine. The Psychiatric

Institute then formed part of the General Hospital. In the spring of 1906 I began to attend his course and became personally acquainted with him. He was then fifty years old, still youthful, a man of medium build with a full dark beard, his hair parted on the left side, his eyes calm and understanding. His movements were quick and energetic, and he would sit down at the desk and begin to talk in an easy fashion in colloquial speech – a manner that brings to mind the fireside chats of today. He often had his own books open before him, but he talked freely and seldom glanced at his text. Never have I seen a greater contrast than that which existed between his easy way of expressing himself and his inexorable destruction of so many outmoded doctrines. When he spoke, for example, about his interpretation of dreams, which had put an end to all academic psychology of the day, he commented: 'These gentlemen do not yet know what has happened to them. They continue fighting like the giant in Ariosto's *Orlando Furioso* who, although decapitated, does not notice it in the heat of the battle and continues to strike.'

The big auditorium was empty. Some twelve to twenty people clustered around the desk in the extreme foreground. Later this changed considerably: the same auditorium was packed every Saturday evening until Freud abruptly discontinued his lectures in 1923 because of his operation.[4] In 1906 we were a peculiar little crowd. What can you expect of apostles? Christianity emerged from a stable; psychoanalysis was first presented to a heterogeneous group of whom only half were physicians like myself. Whatever one may say against us, this much is true: we saw the brilliance of this star of Bethlehem whereas others were blind to it for a long time to come. One of us there used to trim his fingernails with a pocket knife, from time to time, blowing the dust away. Another looked like a Spanish inquisitor, his lips glowing red in the thicket of a black beard. He used to nod like a mandarin while the ceiling light played on his bald head.

Freud used the Socratic method in asking questions. I remember one person who waited for such questions as the hunter for his prey and answered them with infallible correctness. I often felt annoyed, because he knew everything immediately while I had to think and even then often did not know the answer; I was jealous. Anyway, we all agreed that a booklet of not more than one hundred pages, *Three Essays on the Theory of Sexuality*, would sooner or later provoke a mighty change in the thoughts of men. This has happened in part, but more is still to come. Right now, after the man's death, strong tendencies work against Freud's enlightenment. I know now, however, as I did thirty years ago, that a strong impulse for the liberation of mankind will originate from his libido theory.

The first fruits of my acquaintance with Freud's doctrine were a number of short stories, in which I used some of the new psychology, pretty much unknown to most people in those days. I mixed a sarcastic vein with my hobby, the history of Vienna, invented a story and spiced it with 'Freudian mechanisms'. Later, many authors were influenced by the great magician, but I was among the first. There was a story about Napoleon in Vienna and about Barbara, a girl who came to Schönbrunn castle to get his autograph (she got it and more besides). The new theory of the unconscious enabled me to show that Barbara, without consciously intending it, wished to become Napoleon's mistress. Far from being in disgrace, her experience made her famous. The stories, as can be seen, were rather frivolous. Another one of them introduced Ladislaus, a young king in the fifteenth century, who summons a young matron to his palace.[5] When she arrives, he cannot make love to her because something – unknown to him – reminds him of his mother. This is Freud's incest motive, well known to educated people now, but not so well known thirty years ago. I did my best to make the doctrine of 'Freudian slips' a factor in literature. My best did not amount to much, though, as I was unknown then as an author. But since I was a physician as well as a writer, both of these activities now came into play.

3

Kraus and the Neue Freie Presse

Turn-of-the-century Vienna, like every great metropolis, had its leading daily newspaper, the *Neue Freie Presse*, which was quite an institution in those days. It dominated not only the financial world of bankers, brokers and big business, but also the arts. No book, or play or piece of music was a success unless this paper sanctioned it. It seems to me, though I may be wrong, that no paper endowed with such power has done more harm than the *Neue Freie Presse*. The trouble was not that the paper was bad; on the contrary, it was too good. It had critics of superior qualifications, who used the most refined language to annihilate an author. There was, for instance, the famous music expert Edward Hanslick, who tried to subdue Richard Wagner. It was not Hanslick's fault, nor that of the *Neue Freie Presse*, that Wagner's music conquered the world. In rereading today what this critic had to say about *Tristan and Isolde*, one can hardly believe one's eyes. According to him, it was the end of all music, a mind gone astray and even worse. It is well known that Wagner avenged himself in his *Meistersinger* – the revenge of a genius indeed – and that he initially intended to call the figure of the quibbling Beckmesser 'Hans Lick'. Later, Hanslick applied the same form of torture to another great composer, Anton Bruckner. In literature Max Nordau, a man with an erudite pen and cyclopic lack of sense, tried particularly to destroy Ibsen, Nietzsche, Tolstoy and Zola, in short, all the pathfinders of the future. Since these critics wrote so well, it was a real pleasure for conservative spirits to get such excellent service.

Art and literature were not the chief departments of the paper. Moriz Benedikt, the owner and editor, wrote enormous editorials in the financial and political sections for the Bourbons who had turned Manchester liberals, including a weekly column on the stock exchange. Rumours that the man and the paper

12. Moriz Benedikt, editor of the *Neue Freie Presse* (photomontage by Karl Kraus).

were not entirely honest never died. We youngsters had no money, did not care for it and did not concern ourselves at all with politics or economics, at least not in 1900. So whether they were corrupt or not did not make much difference to us. We laughed at the dithyrambic style Benedikt used in writing about such mundane matters as securities and financial manoeuvres. We laughed for years when he overplayed his hand by writing: 'With Godfrey of Bouillon we cry, the rate of interest is with us!' Or when, to stigmatize the antiquated methods of British politics, he started an editorial with the words: 'There are no bathrooms in 10 Downing Street.'

Certainly, the theory of thesis and antithesis applies here, since the *Neue Freie Presse* created its own nemesis in the form of Karl Kraus, a satirical writer who for a long time made it his main business to attack the newspaper and its contributors. We would all read the daily and then look for the delightful travesties, criticisms and witticisms in Kraus's magazine, *The Torch* [*Die Fackel*]. He died in 1936 and the magazine he began in 1899 died with him. It is safe to call him Nestroy's worthy successor; indeed, he is just as little known outside Austria as Nestroy. Someone called him the H. L. Mencken of Vienna, but I do not think the comparison contributes to an understanding of Kraus.

13. Karl Kraus, photo by D'Ora Benda, 1908.

DIE FACKEL

HERAVSGEBER:

KARL KRAVS.

ERSCHEINT DREIMAL
IM MONAT.

PREIS 10 Kr.   WIEN.

14.   Kraus's magazine *Die Fackel* (early cover design).

There is virtually nothing in New York, or in all America in fact, comparable to his relationship to the newspaper which he hated and hunted. The *New York Times*, comparable to the *Neue Freie Presse* in literary authority, is much too impersonal, too encyclopaedic, to call forth an intimate enemy. The *New York Times*, too, is often hated and abused, there are always clashing points of view, but most of these critics refrain, as a rule, from personal references directed at individual editors. It is not easy to imagine one individual who, like a terrier, sank his teeth into an individual editor and would not let loose for many years. Vienna, at the turn of the century, was a gossipy place, the editors were known and everyone liked to watch and enjoy the fun when Joe scuffled with George.

Benedikt took his cause – the cause of German liberal capitalism – with intense seriousness, or pretended to. Kraus tried to unhorse him with tremendous roars of laughter which sometimes rose to the heights of Voltaire in his attacks against the Church. Voltaire's success was only partial; he could not destroy the Church. But Kraus had no practical success at all. We knew beforehand that the *Neue Freie Presse* served the stock exchange and we read the paper just the same. For a long time Kraus considered it his mission to enlighten the world about this newspaper, and Vienna read his stuff because he was very witty indeed. But no one ceased to read a paper to which he was accustomed and for which there was no equivalent substitute. It may even be that reading the paper became more interesting because one anticipated Kraus, who would make a Punch and Judy show of the loftiness and sublime pathos of the *Neue Freie Presse* in his own magazine *The Torch*. We got rid of a good deal of tension and spite in seeing how he pricked Benedikt and his collaborators. After a while Kraus himself admitted that he got nowhere against the paper except in one direction – he succeeded in infuriating the folks in the editorial office in the Fichtegasse. That, he said, meant something, too. It would appear that he started his fight at the wrong end; later leaders of the German nation could have shown him how to accomplish his ends – the *Neue Freie Presse* collapsed and silently disappeared after Hitler marched into Vienna.

In spite of his eccentric theories, Kraus was right and humane in his practical aims. In those days he followed a number of criminal lawsuits attentively and wrote flaming articles in the interests of persecuted women. An executive in a small town committed suicide, and when his case was examined it became obvious that the gossip of the smalltowners had forced him to his death. He was married to a woman with a past, and it seems that his attractive wife remained flirtatious even after her marriage. The widow appeared as witness and fought a verbal duel with the lawyers and the judge. Madame Hervay (for that was her name) claimed emphatically that her private life was her own affair and concerned no one but herself. Kraus, who had

never seen Madame Hervay before, broke a lance in her defence
in his magazine. To be sure, when she later came to thank him
he felt quite embarrassed. She was very much the coquette on
her way back, and as far removed from Thaïs or Aspasia as the
earth from the sun.

At another time a house of assignation was raided, and the
police found out that quite a few members of the best families,
a former police commissioner among them, had been distinguished guests of the brothel. The procuress and the girls
were sent to jail; the names of the guests, however, were
covered with the cloak of Christian love. This stimulated Kraus
to shoot at them with all the acid of his satire. He allowed no
pertinent event to pass without scrutiny, and he fought for
honesty and against the double standard in sex matters whenever
he could. His essays were later collected in several volumes, one
of them called *Sittlichkeit und Kriminalität* (Morality and Criminal
Justice) and another *Die chinesische Mauer* (The Chinese Wall). He
maintained, above all, that women should be entitled to the
same liberty in satisfying their sex urges as men. In addition, he
held that nobody has the right to pry into the private life of his
fellow man. He fought for this second principle even more
strongly than for the first; the sex made no difference to him. In
1907 the political writer, Maximilian Harden publicly blasted
the homosexual clique surrounding the German Kaiser. Kraus
discharged several virulent articles against Harden because, he
maintained, it was nobody's business to find out whether any
dignitary was homosexual or not, whether his orgies were
celebrated with chorus girls or with the white pants of the
Prussian guard. Every theme Kraus took up was scored with
derision, and also with the prophetic gesture: 'Ye have heard
through the *Neue Freie Presse* . . . But I say unto you . . .'

In surveying the life and work of a Karl Kraus, it would seem
that the proverb *Nemo propheta in patria sua* (No one is a great
man in his own country) must often be wrong. Every cultural
centre, even a village, has its own prophet who enjoys the
highest authority at home, unknown though his name might be
but a few miles outside this circle. Kraus was such a local
prophet, writing in a local idiom impossible to translate. The
idiom of Vienna was a kind of Sinhalese for the other parts of
Europe. Kraus was not even understood in the German Reich
outside of Austria, because he was rooted entirely in Vienna's
cultural life, nay, more – one could even say in the inner
city. There are some excellent writers in New York who find

their audience in only a thin layer of sophisticated Broadway, where they direct the subtleties of their pens. By their very confinement to their locality and their day they fascinate within their own circle. The storytellers in the Oriental bazaars are similar.

Kraus was myopic and his angry blue eyes looked through a sharp pince-nez into the world which his straight, pointed nose pierced. There was some resemblance to Karl Radek, the witty agent of the Soviets, who vanished from the world's stage a few years ago. Kraus had to hide a slight kyphosis, the result of infantile rickets. Vienna understood in the age of Freud and Alfred Adler that this inferiority of body drove him to fight as Thersites against the Homeric heroes, although his enemies of the *Neue Freie Presse* could hardly be compared with Achilles and Patroclus. Kraus came of a well-to-do family: his father was a paper manufacturer in Bohemia, his brothers devoted themselves to business, his sisters married businessmen. Only Karl deviated – or rather, in another sense, did not deviate, because Viennese authors frequently were the younger sons of successful business-men. The older sons took over their fathers' businesses, the younger ones became writers. I have not seen any parallel situation in America. In Vienna it was almost customary in both directions: from industry to art or letters and the reverse. The famous Dr Skoda's nephew founded the modern ammunition plant in Czechoslovakia and one of Rokitansky's sons became a prominent opera singer. Arthur Schnitzler was the son of a distinguished laryngologist, Stephan Zweig's father was a successful textile industrialist, Hugo von Hofmannsthal came from a banker's family. Authors less favoured by fortune sometimes assumed that the *Neue Freie Presse* was involved in the début of well-to-do authors, but of course there was no evidence for that. They believed that the fathers advertised and thus made the names of the sons familiar to the newspaper. We did not know then how the powers of talent, perseverance, wealth and social contacts intertwine.

The case of Kraus is the exception that confirms the rule. He showed remarkable journalistic gifts from the beginning, and it seemed almost inevitable that sooner or later he would became an editor of the *Neue Freie Presse*, where his father's firm advertised. But it was his Oedipus complex which interfered and redirected him.[1] He hated fathers, authorities, frozen dignity and the Jews, although he was one himself. There were many Jews in those days who flirted with anti-Semitism, the cannibalistic origin of which they did not see. A paranoiac mechanism was at work in them. It was just as if they said: 'I cannot be a hateful and offensive Jew for, behold, I hate them myself.' This mechanism can still be seen in operation to this very day.

We younger authors loved Kraus as an iconoclast, a fighter against sham and affectation. His witty comments were the talk of the town. We even helped him, whenever he let us, in his practical jokes against the *Neue Freie Presse*. Once he smuggled a long advertisement into the paper, the initial words of each line of which formed the sentence: 'This is a newspaper which would do anything for money.' One day he devised a new method of annoying the paper which later became a kind of Viennese indoor sport. The purpose of the game – in New York they call it a 'plant' – was to make the publisher print letters to the editor which, while seeming important and expert comment on current events, were in reality utter nonsense. A slight earthquake once occurred in the neighbourhood of Vienna, a rarity in this district, and for many weeks the paper was full of descriptions and letters from subscribers *ad nauseaum*. One of these letters came from Kraus, under a pseudonym, of course.[2] As a technical engineer from Moravia, seemingly an expert, he reported that a few minutes before the earthquake the mining–dogs (these are pushcarts on rails used in the coal mines) became restless and barked loudly. The city laughed for a long time at such buffoonery and the editors were furious. For years the 'mining-dogs' were popular in Vienna; people sent nonsensical letters to the papers, and when they appeared in print, *The Torch* was the place where the exposure was triumphantly made public. These 'plants' served a special purpose in revealing the psychology of the editors. We learned to know their blind spots, caused by their different political passions. The workers' daily was always willing to publish complaints against idle or cruel capitalists, while the *Neue Freie Presse* was especially favourable to socialites and aristocrats.

One of Kraus's intimates ordered stationery with the blue insignia of a count and signed his 'letter to the editor' of the *Neue Freie Presse* as 'Countess Dobronowska'. The distinguished lady wrote: 'I wish to tell you about the origin of the pianist Paderewski's name. One of my ancestors lived in St Petersburg at the time of Catherine the Second. Her Majesty had in her retinue a master of ceremonies whose name was Rewski. This Rewski invented a new dance which he exhibited at one of the court balls. The Tzarina was so pleased that she exclaimed "Pas de Rewski, how charming!'' And from that time on Rewski, who happened to be the great-great-great-grandfather of the famous virtuoso, was called Paderewski.' The *Neue Freie Presse* fell for it and printed this nonsense prominently. The shouts of joy in *The Torch* were followed by dignified silence in the daily. It is well nigh incredible what one could insinuate to an editor by playing on his pet emotions, and this not only applies to anti-Semitic papers, which printed every stupidity as long as it was derogatory to the Jews, but is also true of the shrewdest editors of the most intelligent newspapers. This sport was not without a deeper meaning, for it opened the eyes of the public to the rigidity and automatic glibness of a professed allegiance.

Kraus called the press the canker of the world and claimed that it debased our language with its 'journalese'. He targeted the practice of disguising paid advertisements as editorial comment or factual reporting. Genius, he held, was persecuted and the philosophy of yesteryear was employed to kill the living and struggling spirit of the day. In short, according to Kraus, the battle against the press was the battle of God. Kraus could quote great men who had preached the same gospel before him and, since much that he said was based in fact, he might have succeeded in his struggle had not his origin and education deprived him of the ability to recognize the role of the press as just one of the results of our social system. He had little interest in the social struggle which was even then at work in Vienna and elsewhere. He smelled the rotten odour of the system of which the *Neue Freie Presse* was a cardinal exponent, but he did not know that the surgeon's scalpel had to be applied elsewhere. Not in moral accusations nor in aesthetics was any help to be hoped for, but in economics and in fraternity, of which there is not much even in our time. Kraus's own father, like Benedikt, owed his success to a system which Kraus never fought whole-heartedly because he was brought up in it and loved it in spite of his revolutionary attitude. At bottom, he admired the paper which he attacked; one more instance of ambivalence.

For a short time Kraus became my best friend, and for a long time following my best enemy. I saw him for the last time in 1910 and I know only from hearsay what course his life took after that. He concocted poems and aphorisms *à la* Rochefoucauld, and he became, as well, a very successful master of the music halls, where he recited his own works and those of other authors. The *Neue Freie Presse*, however, continued to be the target for the majority of his shafts, and he persisted as stubbornly as Hitler who, in spite of war and glory and world conquest, still persecutes the Jews. The First World War called forth Kraus's aggression in its fullest fury, and here it was directed against an object big enough to account for real hatred. Hence Kraus was at his best and reached hitherto untouched heights. He found the strongest words to use against war. Although he held the *Neue Freie Presse* responsible for the war, he spared neither generals nor the stupid, cowardly petty-bourgeois in his scathing denunciations. Unfortunately, he had little understanding of the economic and social forces which lead to wars, knew nothing of the sinister tendencies within man himself which drive him to death. But he wrote with magnificent force in his semi-dramatic work, *The Last Days of Mankind*. There is apparent in this writing a love of mankind which, as a rule, he carefully concealed.

After the war he travelled in Austria and Germany on lecture tours, but he continued to live in Vienna where everybody knew him. He took more and more interest in language and, like H. L. Mencken, became one of the most penetrating critics of style and grammar. His coterie was always small, but he fascinated them. His followers knew his poems by heart, and women kissed the doorhandle he had touched on leaving. As he would not stand for empty seats, he usually chose the medium-sized and smaller halls, but these very frequently. He could fill them as often as he wished. His small but absolutely unshakeable group did not make a prepossessing appearance; they were malcontents, negativists, impotent iconoclasts whose dictator he was. I myself could never quite accept Kraus as genuine, but I have known many people, competent and critical, in whose judgement Kraus ranked high as author, actor and journalist.

When Hitler came to power in Germany, Kraus's followers expected strong words from him against the man from Upper Austria. But he was no longer able to find them. He used to say sadly: 'With regard to Hitler, my mind is on strike' (*Mir fällt zu Hitler nichts ein*).[3] This, from the lips of a critic of civilized society, is a tragedy. Kraus died in 1936, just before Hitler's march on Vienna, a bachelor, sixty-three years old; he smoked too many cigarettes, which his arteries could not stand.

4

Spiritual Fathers

Kraus played an important and I might almost say sinister role in my life. We were fond of each other for a while, then we hated each other, and now it is all over. I would prefer to leave it to others to appraise his merits as an author, poet and actor, and limit myself to recording my personal experiences with him. Just when I had about a dozen of my short stories in my folder, Kraus published some historical sketches by August Strindberg in his *Torch*. I decided to get in touch with this terrible man. He was merciless, slaying with his pen almost everyone for whom the *Neue Freie Presse* had praise. Being of a bashful nature, I determined to send him an impudent letter which ran roughly as follows: 'You have published a story by Strindberg. I have quite a few stories at home and I'll be damned if every one of them isn't better than Strindberg's . . .' I enclosed one of my stories with the letter. The trick worked, and his answer came by return of post.[1] 'Your self-assertion, to Strindberg's disadvantage,' he wrote, 'made a bad impression on me. I like your story and will print it.' I continued in the same vein, writing back that this story was not my best, rather one of the weaker ones. 'Send me your best,' he replied. I sent a few more and he took them all for publication. I wrote that I wanted to see him, but he answered that right now he had no time for me. Then I explained to him that I was not primarily an author but a scientist, and sent him a paper on birth control which I had just written.

It was a personal experience that led me, in the summer of 1906, to think about the section of the penal code dealing with 'criminal' abortion. I wrote a treatise based on Freud's discoveries and Kraus's philosophy, which at that time I considered in line with Freud's. Birth control was never publicly discussed, and fear of pregnancy poisoned all sex life, even in wedlock, to a degree that led, as Freud taught us, to neurosis,

Wien, *16. Dezember* 1906

Sehr geehrter Herr,
Ihr Brief mit seiner sicheren Selbstein-
schätzung zu Ungunsten Strindberg's
weckte mir kein günstiges Vorurteil für die
Arbeit, die ihm beilag. Sie gefällt mir
aber – zumal in der Stimmung – recht gut,
und ich bin geneigt, sie in dieser oder der
nächsten Nummer der 'Fackel' zu drücken.
Ich bitte Sie mir jedenfalls mitzutheilen,
wann Ihr Buch erscheint. Immerhin müßten
einige Wochen zwischen der Publikation in
der 'Fackel' und der Buchausgabe liegen.
Auch ob Sie schon irgendwo etwas veröf-
fentlicht haben, würde mich interessieren.
Zu persönlicher Besprechung fehlt mir leider
jetzt die Zeit.

In vorzüglicher Hochachtung
Karl Kraus

The text of Kraus's letter, with the original German followed by an English translation.

Vienna, 16 December 1906

Dear Sir,
Your letter with its confident self-assessment to Strindberg's disadvantage did not awaken in me any positive predisposition for the work which accompanied it. However, the work strikes me as rather good, especially in its atmosphere, and I am inclined to print it in the forthcoming or the following number of the 'Torch'. I ask you in any case to inform me when your book will appear. After all there would have to be several weeks between publication in the 'Torch' and the book edition. It would also interest me to know whether you have already published anything anywhere. Unfortunately I do not at the moment have time for a personal discussion.

Yours faithfully
Karl Kraus

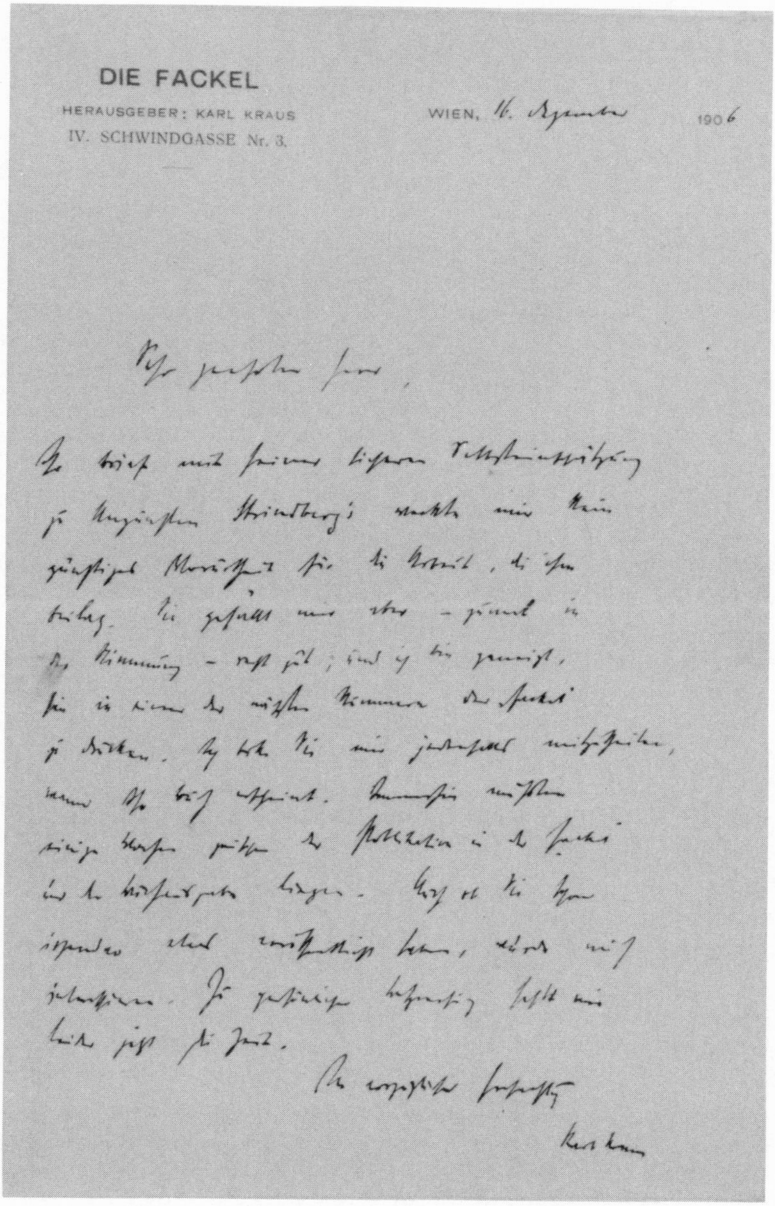

DIE FACKEL

HERAUSGEBER: KARL KRAUS
IV. SCHWINDGASSE Nr. 3.

WIEN, *16. Dezember* 1906

15.   Facsimile of Kraus's first letter to Wittels, 16 December 1906.

alcoholism and even crime. The prohibition of abortion was responsible for the murder of newborn infants. Particularly disgusting was the difference in treatment accorded the poor, who were sent suffering to prison while the well–to–do were attended by prominent abortionists and breathed the fragrance of flowers on the bedside tables. I remember the strongest passage of the essay: 'If they really wish to do something against abortion, let them fight starvation and the fear of it. They cannot prohibit what their very existence forces people to do. But this is not the worry of the legislators. The church needs babies to christen, the generals need cannon fodder and the factories need the unemployed who keep the wages down.' One could not speak about these conditions in early post–Victorian times, certainly not in the *Neue Freie Presse*. A physician risked his future even by signing such an article. So I chose as my *nom de plume* the name of the old Arabian doctor Avicenna, and sent my comprehensive work to Kraus. He seemed to like it and published it early in 1907.

When Kraus published my essay on birth control under the sensational title 'The Greatest Crime in the Penal Code', Freud approached me after his lecture and said: 'Did you write this? It is like a brief and I subscribe to every word of it.'[2] With this he invited me to join his group, which met weekly in his office. This was certainly a great honour and, as I dare confess now, an undeserved one. I abused Freud's theory, believing that his mission was to lead us to a free, unrestricted sex life. I considered him a scholar who forged the weapons with which Kraus and I would tear to bits a world of hypocrisy and hysteria. Freud is a liberator and will live as such through the centuries. But he had no use for the ideal of Kraus at all, this ideal being just as neurotic as sex denial.

Overnight I had become a power in Vienna. All the young questioning intellectuals and their circles began to respect me as a contributor to *The Torch*, which Karl Kraus, as a rule, wrote himself almost in its entirety. Likewise, from that day on, I was impossible in the *Neue Freie Presse*. Through this article I met Kraus personally, and from then on I had two spiritual fathers, of whom only one has attained international fame. In my opinion they were the two champions of sexual liberty in our city. I could not then see the tremendous difference between a true scientist and a propagandizing journalist, eloquent writer though he was. Freud actually became a liberator of suppressed sex life – this was his destiny – but, in a sense, without or even contrary to his will. Copernicus did not mean to attack the Church with his discoveries, yet the Church felt itself attacked and struck back. Freud never assumed a fencer's attitude, yet almost all took him for a swordsman. I remember a lecture which Freud gave about that time in a student fraternity. The problem was whether sexual abstinence before marriage was advisable or not. In those days venereal diseases were supposed to be fought by education, and prominent physicians advised 'chastity' as the best hygiene against syphilis. Freud said he could not believe that nature had endowed man with sex organs for the purpose of not using them. 'If,' he said, 'there is really no other way to prevent venereal diseases, all right, then abstain, but – abstain under protest.' 'Isn't it terrible!' exclaimed the old women of both sexes. 'He told the youngsters to proceed straightway to the whore house.'

One can understand that under those circumstances an investigator not shrinking from the consequences of his doctrine could be taken for a sexual revolutionary. In reality Freud did not like Kraus's extravagances at all. The ballyhoo of the Viennese coffee-houses increased the general resistance to psychoanalysis as psychological and medical research. There was little understanding in the coffee-houses of anxiety hysteria and compulsion neurosis, whereas they proclaimed an imminent revolution in our sexual mores, of which Freud, strictly conventional in his private life, would have preferred to hear as little as possible. He was an investigator, not a reformer. Yet, as he said himself, he had to fulfil his destiny and was not in a position to select his own apostles, of whom I was one of the loudest.

No sooner had I made the acquaintance of Kraus than he drew me into the whirl of his private life. I still lived in the General Hospital and worked there from morning to evening. Kraus got up late in the afternoon and wandered about the coffee-houses till late at night. His satirical assaults were written very late, as a rule, in the small hours of the morning. We had so much to discuss! At four o'clock in the morning he saw me home, and at the door of the hospital we turned around and I saw him back – not home, because it was too early for that, but to some coffee-house in which his companions waited for him, ready to laugh at his malicious witticisms. (They did not drink there, in the coffee-houses; Kraus never took a drop of liquor.) With me he was serious. We spoke about women. He explained how women in our time had to live against their nature. They could all be

beautiful, and some day to come they would be as they were in
the sunny civilization of ancient Greece.

I am afraid that in the course of my friendship with Kraus,
who became ever more important to me, I neglected my medical
duties. One has to sleep some time. My case histories grew
careless and my teacher, Dr Kovacs, lost a good deal of his
confidence in me. I left his department of internal medicine and
continued in Wagner-Jauregg's Psychiatric Institute as resident
second assistant. It was clear by then that psychiatry would have
to become my speciality. Wagner-Jauregg was opposed to
psychoanalysis, as were most of his assistants. They scorned me
and I scorned them. This, in addition to my chronic need of
sleep, was none too good for my psychiatric education. I had to
make up for that later.

Kraus turned my head by emphasizing that I had by now – I
was twenty-six – become one of the greatest writers of
Germany. This appraisal, coming from one of the most dreaded
critics, impressed me deeply. He probably meant – the best after
himself. He spoke of me in the same vein to his friends, but they
did not agree with him and looked at me askance. I wrote one
article after another for *The Torch*, psychological short stories,
too, and my essays actually grew better and certainly bolder. I
was successful, my self-confidence increased and I got the best
out of myself.

I was then one of the few who understood Freud's discoveries,
and among those few perhaps the only one who could write. I
often made use of Freud in my own way and applied
psychoanalysis in a polemical spirit, although Freud even then
warned us all against provoking and engaging in polemics. But
how could one be Kraus's collaborator and not attack! I wrote an
article against women studying medicine, based in part on
Kraus's philosophy that women had to limit themselves to being
sex creatures exclusively, and in part on Freud's theory of the
displacement of affects.[3] I said that girls came to medical schools
under the pretext of studying but actually in a kind of unfair
competition for the purpose of attracting men. This actual
tendency, I said, was unknown to them; I evidently thought
myself chosen to make it conscious to them. Behind their
professed aim I dug out bisexuality, exhibitionism, peeping and
whatever more I could find in the armoury of psychoanalysis.
This adolescent outpouring of a revengeful psychologist in the
making took no account of social drives, and, while it was well
and forcefully written, or rather because of that, it created

indignation in the hospital and even in Freud's own circle. In the coffee-houses it was received with enthusiasm.

Freud's followers gathered every Wednesday in his home (the details of these gatherings I have described in my book, *Sigmund Freud*).[4] At the meeting following my publication I was severely attacked. In those days, Alfred Adler, who later founded a school of psychology of his own, was the most prominent member of the Freudian circle. He smoked long, thin Virginia cigars incessantly and spoke the slow-going Viennese idiom with conviction. He said, 'We owe it to our young confrère to tell him in all frankness what we think of his latest opus.' After this ominous introduction all of them pounced upon me, except Freud himself, who at that time favoured me and smiled inwardly at my firing back at them.[5] Yet I learned later that he had ordered this punitive expedition. In the hospital a colleague who was in love with one of the girl doctors challenged me to a duel, which the superintendent foiled by threatening to kick us both out.

There is something ironic about this article against women doctors, inasmuch as I have changed my mind completely and for many years have been in favour of them. I love intelligent women who eventually may beat one in argument; but most men harbour a slight grudge against them, whether they admit it or not. Because of this change in my attitude, I frequently found myself in the awkward position of having to refute my own article before people who found my discarded arguments very forceful. Among them were quite a number of women. Their emancipation, won by women in broad, low-heeled shoes, had ended in the universality of lipstick, high heels and the freedom of the sea beaches. It is by now clear to anybody that girls in lecture halls introduce a kind of sexual stimulation into rooms where the old church motto had hitherto been valid: *mulier taceat in ecclesia* (the woman has no voice in the congregation). Hence puritans, sometimes even those of the Marxian brand, are against women in medicine, while I feel that young men should be happy to breathe feminine fragrance while they are shown the lugubrious exhibits of our medical school. My article against medical women was a 'masculine protest' dictated by fear. History has passed over all these neurotic complexes.

A few days after I first met Kraus, we became fast friends. I was twenty-six and he was seven years older. We met every evening for dinner in the Red Hedgehog [Der rote Igel], a restaurant behind the opera house. From there we walked to the

16. Berggaße 19, scene of Freud's Wednesday evening meetings (later the Vienna Psychoanalytic Society).

Café Pucher on the Kohlmarkt. Later we would go to Café Frohner in the building of the Hotel Imperial, now known as Hitler's first residence in Vienna. From the Frohner we went down to the lower-class cafés patronized by prostitutes and bookies. Kraus said he needed this change of atmosphere so as to get rid of the bourgeois slime which polluted the better cafés. In the small hours of the morning he went home and worked on his articles, apothegms and poems until seven or eight in the morning, after which he went to bed and slept a good part of the day. He called this the only intelligent way of living. I tried to match his intelligence in this respect, but I had to go home to my hospital and begin work shortly after eight. My libido was split between Kraus and medicine, and I am afraid that I began to neglect my medical duties.

Much has been said about Vienna's cafés. There are cafés in France and in Italy, but they are not the same. The Vienna coffee-house is a spacious place, modestly decorated, furnished with oblong and round marble tables (no tablecloth under any circumstances!), upholstered benches and comfortable chairs. Billiard tables and an opportunity for playing cards, chess and checkers are provided in the thick air, filled with tobacco smoke, but no music. All the guests were known to the waiters, and if

17. *Whirlwind in the Coffeehouse*, sketch by an unidentified artist (possibly A. P. Gütersloh).

one of them was not known, why he became known as a stranger. The patrons came and left at the same time every day. Order had to prevail. Whenever possible they used the same table, which, for such distinguished guests as Mr Kraus, would be reserved. Politicians, gamblers, businessmen, opera singers, jockeys, all had their reserved tables. Nothing of the kind exists in America or was ever even attempted. They say it would not pay here and they are right. It would not pay because one cannot transplant the spirit of the coffee-house, which comes from the Near East and is the spirit of the Oriental Bazaar. There a man does his business, meets his friends, listens to gossip, fairy tales and music, sits down for his innumerable little cups of black coffee. The indescribable and inimitable loveliness of the coffee-house must be linked to the Arabian nights. The Prussian goose-step and the Viennese coffee-house are mutually exclusive.

Kraus's system of wandering from one café to another was not at all typical of Vienna. Most of us patronized just one place regularly. When after my first year in the States I came back home, the head waiter of my café asked me with reserved indignation: '*Herr Doktor*, where have you been? Haven't seen you in ages.' When I explained that I came from America, he winked his eye, which meant: 'You can't fool me. You simply were in another café and nostalgia drove you back.' When I stayed away another year he gave me up and looked away when

I came again. No matter where I'd been in the meantime, I was a traitor. How can a real Viennese desert his city?

Two gentlemen were always to be seen in Kraus's company, while others joined them from time to time. Kraus was exceedingly witty, and when he had one of his good days he enchanted us all. Attractive girls, actors and artists, high officials, critics, all kinds of people came to his table, and he made us feel we were the centre of the universe. Some of the very people he attacked in the last issue of *The Torch* came to sit with him. At other times he was so moody that no one could stand him. Then he would sit alone, but never quite alone, because the two gentlemen, and for some time myself as the third, were always with him. One of them was Polish, a man called Pawlikowski or Pomiankowski or something of the sort [Ludwig von Janikowski].[6] He lived on a nice sinecure, which the Polish Secretary for Transportation had granted him. He was a librarian in the Ministry of Transportation, where he sat at his desk in the centre of a large room filled with books which no human ever entered. He spent his evenings with Kraus. He admired him beyond limits and sometimes borrowed money from him. In Kraus's opinion the Pole was one of the finest specimens of humankind.

The other gentleman, Karl Hauer, formerly an elementary school teacher, had lost his job on account of his radical views.[7] He was small, thin and silent, with a bitter obstinacy around his mouth, as though he meant to express: 'As long as things do not change for the better, I won't open my mouth.' When I joined them, these two did not like me. I took too much of Kraus's libido away from them. Hauer, the schoolteacher, published good essays in *The Torch*. His radicalism was entirely anarchistic, no thinkable order of things suited him. He was against everything except an unrestricted sex life, and that only in theory. Kraus had the bad habit of calling waiters names. To Hauer goes the credit for stopping that for good. He said to Kraus in his sad, slow way: 'The waiter can't answer back. But nothing in the world can prevent him from spitting in your soup outside.'

Pawlikowski and Hauer would patronize me by regarding me as a normal man. Once we were discussing marriage and Kraus said I should never marry. Kraus himself and the other two were bachelors. Pawlikowski said, and I will never forget the disdain in his voice, 'Why shouldn't he? He's an absolutely normal human being.' Kraus upheld my side, and not only did I learn his ideas on women and sex, but I soon became his practical collaborator. It was through Kraus that I met Irma, seventeen years old, the youngest daughter of a janitor in the suburbs of Vienna.[8] Kraus was so enthusiastic about her that he nominated her a late-born Greek, a hetaera.[9] For me she became the 'child woman'.

5

The Child Woman

Kraus was by nature a puritan. For a long time two of his older friends, Adolf Loos, father of modern architecture and interior decoration, and Peter Altenberg, the Verlaine of Vienna, tried in vain to prove to him not only that sexual freedom for women was desirable, but also that only the sexually emancipated woman can be a real help to the creative man. Kraus was against it until he met Annie Kalmar, a beautiful actress who took him by storm. She was promiscuous, passionate, gay, careless, a drunkard, intelligent without being educated. From then on Kraus was a changed man. Suddenly he realized the truth of his friends' words. Just the same, his puritanical nature challenged him and in this conflict he became quite a violent preacher of the gospel of the whore. He even dared to publish an article 'In Praise of the Whore'. After a short springtime of love, Annie, his hell-fire, died of pneumonia and Kraus almost died with her. She hadn't lived long enough to show him the unbearable other side of the medal. When he recovered from the shock of her death, his new philosophy of sex and women was ready, like Buddha's on the eightfold way. According to Kraus, women not only had the right but it was their bounden duty to be whores. All women who did not conform to this were neurotics and enemies of civilization.

About a year before I met him, Kraus saw a girl on the streets of Vienna who struck him by her resemblance to his beloved Annie. She was only a torso of his ideal, he said, using the word in an unusual way. What he meant was that Irma had the features, hair and eyes of Annie, but not her figure. Irma was petite, Annie was tall with a free and proud gait, a real Greek hetaera.[1] This difference made Irma no less appealing to Kraus, and he became her lord protector. I may anticipate here and mention that he remained her protector – often against his will –

18. Annie Kalmar, Karl Kraus's first love.

for over twenty-five years, until she died, and I think he will be forgiven all his sins for that.[2] When I first joined the circle, Irma hardly ever appeared. Kraus told me about her, how lovely she was, what a pagan in the Hellenic sense, how free in sexual matters and how unhappy. It was his contention that this ascetic

19. Irma Karczewska: artist's impression by John G. Ramsay.

world throws dirt at creatures it should worship, as they were worshipped in a civilization incomparably higher than our own. Irma was a dream of beauty. He showed me photographs of her with grape leaves and clusters in her black hair and a radiant smile on her parted lips.

In short, I was in love with her, before I ever saw her. Then I met her. She was a mere girl of seventeen, dumb and boring, except in matters of sex. In this sphere she showed a sophistication all the more amazing when compared with her complete lack of interest in anything else. I did not realize that this was Kraus's work, a miracle of a Dionysian girl born several thousand years too late. Hauer once told me that Irma was nothing but an empty shell filled with phrases from *The Torch*, but I did not believe him. He also said that the world was not ascetic at all, but that Kraus was. As a matter of fact Kraus, with all his admiration for her, had no use for Irma any more, and worked hard getting his friends to assume the burden of personal service. He was well-to-do and took lavish care of her financially. She came originally from surburban proletarian stock, but now she wore fur coats, bracelets and everything.

Unfortunately, when I met her she was ill and couldn't leave the house. I would spend the evenings with her, keeping her from drinking excessively and from gallivanting too much. I don't know how many sleepless nights I spent preventing her from proving that she was by nature a Greek maenad. She had to be entertained all the time, had to get a reward for each day she refrained from drinking. The rewards ranged from theatre tickets and money to simply keeping her company, which was perhaps the most difficult thing of all. Kraus liked me more and more. I had become indispensable to him. Usually, I spent the evening with her until she was in bed and asleep, and then, long after midnight, I would join Kraus and his crowd in one of the coffee-houses. I do not pretend she was true to me. This was neither to be expected of a hetaera nor would it even have been desirable. According to theory she could not be and should not be true to anyone.

Since Irma was sick and miserable and I was a physician, I made it my business to cure her. This was quite a task, for which one had to be physician and nurse in one. As long as she was weak and ran a temperature, it was a medical problem like many others; later, when she improved, one needed the energy of a Hercules, the patience of Job and the inventive gifts of Ulysses to prevent her from harming herself by liquor and nightly escapades, and also to persuade her to follow the necessary treatment. In the midst of these difficulties we came quite close to each other; she was like a puppy which at one time looks at you with gratitude, at another bites the dressing off its wound. One had to promise her a gift for every evening that she stayed in and went to bed early: a red azalea in a green pot, caviare, a pair of opera-glasses, an umbrella, a cloth brush with an animal on it, a decanter which could play a melody, theatre tickets, stockings, gloves, brooches of all kinds, and so on *ad infinitum*. Finally she asked me to make Kraus take her with him when he travelled to Italy in the summer. I knew that this was impossible. He was quite generous about her financial demands, purchasing his liberty in this way. I had her all to myself, as far as it is possible to monopolize a 'late-born Greek' who had only one principle: not to have any.

Late in the spring, the son of a Swedish mining baron fell in love with her.[3] He was a silly young man, but not much sillier than we, and he meant to marry her. He knew nothing of Hellas and late-born hetaerae; on the contrary, he saw in Irma an angel of chastity, and that was really what she looked like, young, delicate, virginal. He was jealous of me, but what could he do? I was the doctor. I was probably jealous of him, too, because Irma wavered between myself, who understood the importance of her hetaeristic existence, and the young Swede who, while he did not appreciate her achievements, meant to marry her just because he didn't. He asked her to write to his parents in Sweden so that they could see from her letters that she would make a worthy daughter-in-law. She showed me these letters before sending them, and I saw that they would never do. She copied them from those which a girl friend had sent her sweetheart. The friend had written about all the places where they had been together, and so Irma, too, started one of her letters to the Swedish in-laws-to-be with the words, 'Oh, Bermuda, Oh, the ocean!' I asked her what she meant by these exclamations, and she said she did not know. Her friend had used them in a letter so why shouldn't she? I had to help her with those letters, and maybe one day God will make me responsible for this, because the young man really married her a year or two later and took her north to Sweden. True, she came back after half a year's absence and did not talk about her matrimonial experiences. I suppose that she obtained a divorce.

My friendship with Kraus and my infatuation with his work, not his written work but the one called Irma,[4] a janitor's daughter, inspired me to write a paper published in *The Torch* in 1907: 'The Child Woman'.[5] The idea of the paper concerned a girl of great sexual attraction, which breaks out so early in her life that she is forced to begin her sex life while still, in all other respects, a child. All her life long she remains what she is: oversexed and incapable of understanding the civilized world of adults. Nor does this world understand her. Into this theoretical framework I pressed the floods of my enthusiasm, quoting Helen of Troy, Lucretia Borgia, Manon Lescaut and Zola's Nana. Naturally, using Freud's terms, I explained that this type is necessarily 'polymorphous perverse', sadistic, lesbian and what-not.[6]

Beloved Irmerl, whose knees I passionately embrace in spirit!

Those poor, beautiful, brown knees, which are so often painful. I am already deep in memories again. Everything is dear to me, including things which earlier seemed so unpleasant. How we quarrelled in the Kärntnerstraße at night and you threw the money down at my feet, the cab was waiting round the corner and the whores were watching. And how I dragged you out of Kraus's bed and you said: 'You can love me your whole life long.' And above all the blue geisha-girl bathrobe, hell and damnation, what wonderful hours those were, Monna Vanna! And those noctural visits to the Weyringerstraße where I had to tiptoe so quietly, everything was so incredibly beautiful and more and more beautiful. As I am writing this I am seized by a boundless longing for you. I simply cannot understand that I didn't manage kissing you properly, for it's exactly that I'm longing for most and almost fainting for. For in kissing you are the greatest, as you must well understand after the clumsiness which you observed on my side.

Have you looked through 'The Child Woman'? Everyone is asking me about the model for it, since even those who are not so taken by the article are curious to get to know the original. They realize that the original must be quite something.

When you are on the esplanade and the sun is shimmering over the lake, then think of me and write to say whether I can come. I kiss your ear, your breasts, the birthmark above your left breast and everything else that is as precious as all the treasures of Arabia.

Yours
Fritz

21 July 1907

20. Facsimile of a letter from Wittels to Irma alluding to the 'Child Woman', 21 July 1907, with an English translation.

I must now return from this Bedlam to the great scientist whose disciple I became about this time. One Wednesday night in Freud's circle I read my paper about the child woman. That night I was suffering from lumbago and had a Japanese heat box strapped to the small of my back. Irma had printed her name on it in ink; she was literally glowing behind me while I spoke and psychoanalysed her soul. She had been 'polymorphous perverse' as an infant and had never developed any cultural inhibitions, because from early childhood on she was so much in demand for love that no time was given her for any 'latency'. For the same reason she was the absolute contrast of lush sensuousness: her nature breathed serenity. Since neurosis was a product of repression and conflict, she was the prototype of an un-neurotic soul not fit for our neurotic age. No wonder she was despised and persecuted.

I do not recall now what the others had to say of my performance. Freud was somewhat annoyed and said that the type in question was the perfect ragamuffin (*Haderlump*).[7] He advised me to read my manuscript to him before publication, which, of course, I did one evening in his studio. He was favourably inclined at first and interrupted me with friendly remarks. Soon, however, he could not refrain from letting me see that he did not like my ways. It was not his intention, he said, to lead the world to an uninhibited frenzy. On the contrary, he wished to teach men not to satisfy their instincts in a thousand more or less neurotic disguises. They should consciously decide what to do and what not to do. Instead of repressing and lying to themselves they should consciously reject what they consider evil. They should stop not letting the right arm know what the left arm does. Psychoanalysis as a science could not and would not pronounce upon good and evil. In such decisions he, Freud, could never speak as representative of the science whose creator he was; he was just an individual with personal inclinations. He would like to share these personal inclinations with his pupils, and my tirades, as put forward in *The Torch*, were opposed to his own beliefs in many respects. He had not much use for child women, and counselled me to be more prudent myself. He was not happy about the influence of the editor of *The Torch* on me. We had developed, he said, strange blind spots for the cultural forces to which civilized men have to yield.

After this discussion with the master I mitigated the fury of my revolutionary attitude and published my manuscript in a rewritten shape. It contained one of my more important contributions to analytical psychology: the figure of the 'child woman'.[8] Freud himself fell back on my type later when he formulated his concept of Narcissism: she was the narcissistic woman.[9] We were all narcissistic in those days of intoxication, all who lived in Kraus's atmosphere. We were not tolerant enough to leave women alone; they all had to be and to behave as we dictated. We knew from Freud that repressed sex instincts made men neurotic to such an extent that an entire era was poisoned. What we did not know then was that former puritans running wild would not help either. No civilization is conceivable without limitations of some kind – in the realm of sex, too. Any civilization demands recognition of its institutions of which love, fidelity and devotion are the most valuable. There we were preaching an animalistic promiscuity which we ourselves could not endure in actual life. I am a little ashamed of that phase of my youth for which I had two excuses: the fascinating theories of Kraus and his creation, Irma.

★

When the summer of this eventful year, 1907, came around, Kraus declared that he would rather commit suicide than travel to Italy with Irma. He suggested that I go with her, and I agreed because Irma and I loved one another. The young man had temporarily returned to Sweden and the girl was at large. I had some misgivings about travelling with an ancient Greek girl, and made Kraus promise me that he would arrange his return from Sorrento, Italy, so as to meet us in Venice.[10] Venice was then almost a suburb of Vienna. Budapesters and Viennese met on the Lido in summer as New Yorkers and Chicagoans meet in Florida in winter.

My trip with Irma to this city turned out to be an ordeal, though one of those of which you say later, 'I wouldn't have missed it for anything'. Everything happened as was to be expected and a little worse. I suffered from the girl's temperament which by then I knew: she could be true to one only as long as she obviously needed one. Since she had regained her health, I did not interest her any more. Worse than that, she showed unmistakable antagonism towards me because I foolishly asked of her what she did not have and could not give. If, on the other hand, one takes into account the fact that I was in love with this most attractive misfit, one understands why, in the midst of radiant sunshine, cooing pigeons and serenading tenors, I was deeply depressed in Venice. Love does not live by sex alone.

We left Vienna by night train. That afternoon a wardrobe closet had tumbled over. It was equipped with a drawer at the base and when you pulled it out and stepped on its edge, the entire thing fell on you. Irma acquired a few scratches on her adorable little arm and, being a child in all but sex, felt the urgent need of punishing the closet for bad behaviour. This did not prove satisfactory so she turned on me and tried to kick me in the shins. I might have cancelled the trip. But did I?

Early next morning our train rolled over the plains between Trieste and Venice, later to become a bloody battlefield. We crossed rivers with wide sandy banks: Isonzo, Tagliamento, Brenta. I tried to show her how the rivers, winding through the flat land, could be followed far out to their sun-dusty mouth in the sea. That, I said, makes the land look like a map. She yawned and said: 'All lands look like maps, stupid. Maps are made the way the land looks.' Her injured arm was beginning to get sore.

Over the long bridge across the sea we entered Venice, and I grew sentimental. It is Shakespeare's city and Lord Byron's. Casanova lived there and Richard Wagner died in Palazzo Vendramin. I was glad to be able to come again. Irma, who had never in her life been so far from Vienna, fell into a temper, swore like a dipsomaniac and abused me. She was annoyed because she had to wait for her luggage, because no rooms were free in the beach hotels, because there were so many Jews at the station – she mistook the Italians for Jews – all because her arm hurt and in addition because everything seemed so silly.

We boarded a gondola and zigzagged the lagoons to a hotel. In the summertime, it is a fact, the lagoons smell. Our provisional hotel for the night was in a delightfully narrow street, so narrow that you could touch the buildings on the other side with your outstretched hands. At one end a green canal with refuse floating in it could be seen and behind the canal a barred window with blue stockings and other laundry hanging out to dry. Our hotel room was low, had a stone floor, the door and shutters were rickety, and there was no bath. She looked at me scornfully: 'I won't stay in this dump!'

'It's just for the night. We'll move to the Lido tomorrow.' She did not favour me with a reply, instead she sat down without removing her cloak and began writing a letter.

'Whom are you writing to?'

'None of your business.'

It was my impression that at home one could adore a Greek hetaera born too late, but by no means could one travel with one. I left Irma and walked to the Piazza San Marco, not far away. The church shone in the sun, the sky was blue, a thousand gondolas danced in the sea. Gay crowds of people from every country in the world strolled up and down, but I felt quite depressed. Passing the arcades, I looked into Café Giacomuzzi. Sure enough, Kraus was sitting there, piercing the air with his pointed nose and evidently thinking of new tricks to play on Mr Benedikt of the *Neue Freie Presse* in Vienna. He was agreeably surprised to see me. I complained about the hetaera, expressing my fear that the worst was yet to come. 'Let's send her home,' Kraus suggested. He reckoned without her.

The three of us went to the beach, where the season was in full swing. Siegfried Wagner, Richard's less gifted son, strolled on the sand and absorbed Irma's interest so completely that she had no eyes for the sea at all. She had never seen the sea before, and opinion has it that the blue expanse merging with the horizon, the surf, the air, the breeze are sure to make an everlasting impression on people beholding all this for the first time. This seems to be an error. The late Siegfried Wagner made a stronger impression on Irma when she saw him the first time.

'I say, is this the one who made *Lohengrin*?'

'His son.'

'Who does he go out with?'

He happened to be courting Isadora Duncan, the American dancer, and it took quite some time to explain to Irma how such a thing was possible. Finally, when she was implored to cast at least one glance at the water glittering in the sunshine, she summarized her feelings with the question: 'Any sharks in it?'

I would have preferred one of the smaller Italian villas, but there was the new Hotel Excelsior with some five hundred rooms, with luminous fountains and springs, Moorish arches, Gothic towers and Greek statues. Irma was irresistibly drawn to this hotel. There and nowhere else would she live. So we took two rooms and went down to the beach. I began feeling somewhat better when another event struck me between the eyes. Irma's heels were exceedingly high and the loose sand was deep. One of the heels broke off. A little boy picked it up and brought it to us. The shoe being just as apathetic as the wardrobe closet in Vienna, I had to be punished for this, too. I behaved meekly, put her in one of the bath-houses, took shoe and heel and hot-footed it for a shoe repair. Kraus stayed at her side and tried to make it clear to her that a woman who loses a heel is debased. He, for his part, had to discontinue further contact with such a woman. 'Maybe,' he said, 'if you plead guilty. But an unattractive girl is not guilty either and yet she has to pay for it.' Hence, as I returned with the shoe, I could hear them both yelling from a distance, and finally I had to rescue Kraus from her clawing nails.

The bath-house didn't belong to us, so I asked Irma to put her shoe on quickly and walked ahead with Kraus. We fancied we were alone with no woman with us at all, which seemed a rapturous idea. But we had to walk back for her and found her sitting on the little bench in the bath-house. The shoe was by her side and she stretched out her stockinged foot triumphantly. 'Have no button-hook,' she said. Kraus and I looked at each other with murderous instincts. When she finally came along with us, she smiled and everything was forgiven. You must not forget that little Irma was in our eyes beautiful beyond compare.

Next morning we went sightseeing. San Giovanni e Paolo, the Frari and other churches in Venice are known all over the world. We could not make Irma enter one of them. Churches, she decided, are too dull. We took her to the Academy and promenaded among the Titians, Bellinis and Veroneses. She was bored. Luckily for her she discovered an enormous plaster cast of Hercules in some corner. She was fascinated, and I could not make her move from it. I tried to explain to her that the artistic value of the paintings all around us was infinitely greater than that of the plaster cast, but she insinuated I had personal motives by saying: 'You're just jealous, you're no match for this one.' With this she stepped closer to the statue and examined it so intimately that I pretended to the others in the room that I didn't know her.

We passed a tall English woman in a long cape. Irma asked me to buy her such a cape. I said: 'You are too small for a thing like that.' She took this for an insult and without a word she ran away. I looked for Kraus in the Giacomuzzi, and after a short debate we decided to buy three tickets home. His first plan was to send me home with her while he stayed on in the sunny city a little longer. I made him change his mind. 'Don't you think,' he said, 'hysterica has talent for the stage?' I didn't think so. He thought we might try anyhow. Perhaps we could get her an engagement in Berlin or some other city at least four hundred miles from Vienna.

Oh, Irma, unbearable creature of Periclean times, why have you vanished? The sea is grand, Italy's sky is beautiful and the palaces of Venice awe–inspiring. But you are a hundred times more beautiful than anything in this world. One look at you could save damned souls. You are a golden dream in a forest of red azaleas.

En route back I explained to her that she had spoiled our vacation through her misbehaviour and made her go and apologize to Kraus in the other compartment, where he sat sullenly. She obeyed like a lamb. A few minutes later Kraus stormed out of his refuge and shouted: 'Do you know what she wants? A mahogany baby-grand and I'm to order it for her immediately!' That was her way of apologizing.

★

Kraus frequently voiced in *The Torch* his admiration for the actor Alexander Girardi.[11] When we returned from Venice with our adored plague Irma, I proceeded with her to Ischl, the beautiful mountain spa near Salzburg. Girardi spent his summers there, and the object was to make him recommend Irma to a Berlin theatrical director.

Girardi was undoubtedly one of the greatest artists I ever met; with an apt gesture, an ingenious intonation, a wink of his eye he could make one laugh or cry. With this proviso: one had to be Viennese to be affected. Girardi was always himself whatever role he played. The instant he made his entrance on the stage we would break into boisterous laughter, like children watching the capers of a clown at the circus. The world emulated him and his creations: the vendor of birds, the Hungarian breeder of hogs, the gypsy baron, the sprendthrift nobleman, the humble valet, the philosophical shoemaker. He would introduce his character with a song, a melody which all Vienna would hum and sing following the opening night.

Yet this Girardi, the incomparable craftsman of gaiety, was in his private life melancholic, as is so often the case with professional comedians. He should not have married Helene Odilon, an actress of rare beauty. Their marriage did not end the affair she was having with a prominent financier. Gossips related that Girardi discovered his wife's chemise in her lover's bedroom. Not sharing Kraus's advanced views on women, Girardi threatened to kill both Helene and her financier, the Baron. This led them to complain to the police, and since the authorities could not possibly arrest Girardi, they attempted to

21. The actor Alexander Girardi in the role of Valentin from Raimund's *Der Verschwender*.

commit him to an insane asylum until his agitation subsided. The actor got wind of the plot and fled to the protection of Käthe Schratt, who as former mistress of the old Emperor Franz Joseph wielded considerable influence. She curbed the bailiffs, made Girardi promise to restrain his homicidal instincts, and the result was a hushed–up divorce. I know that all this is malignant gossip, but one cannot understand Vienna without gossip.

The great comedian had already remarried by the time we visited him in Ischl, but the furore of his previous marital

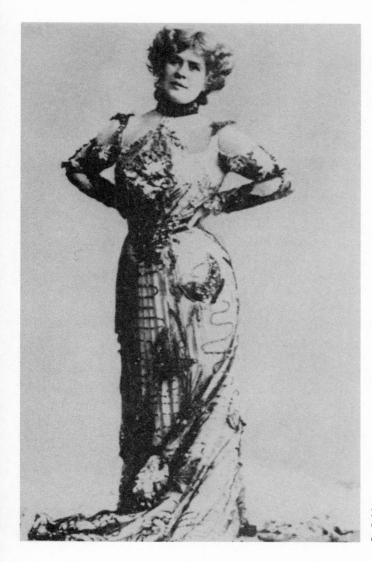

22. The actress Helene Odilon (Girardi's estranged wife).

experience had not yet completely abated. Perhaps Girardi had forgotten, but not Irma. We saw him, he was most cordial but explained that since he was a clown he knew nothing about the stage. Nevertheless, he arranged an audition for Irma with a certain Herr Kren, a famous Berlin director.

'My dear Giri,' said Kren, 'her voice will not carry beyond the music pit!'

'That is precisely why you must develop it,' said Girardi.

'But, dear Giri, she acts atrociously.'

'That's why you must engage her and coach her to act.'

This continued with mounting pressure until Kren, who

depended upon Girardi's box-office attraction, was finally compelled to agree. With Girardi it was a matter of principle. He
wanted to put down a cold-hearted Prussian director whom he
detested (as we all did in those days) by forcing him to engage
this wild child from Vienna. We regarded all Prussians as stuffed
shirts, and it seems as if we had the right slant. Once, when
Kraus and I were strolling along a Berlin thoroughfare, some
fire-engines rattled by. Kraus turned to me and said: 'What's the
use? Do *they* care if their houses burn down?' And later, milling
in the throng: 'Do you think blood would flow if I stabbed one
of these robot machines?'

When we left Girardi's villa, it had started to rain. 'Poor kids,'
he said to us, 'you'll get wet to the chemise.' This was his
version of the more common 'wet to the skin'. Irma took this as
her cue and to my horror replied: 'Do you mean Madame
Odilon's chemise? I know all about that.' Citing this impossible
tactlessness, I am moved to emphasize again how diabolically
appealing Irma was, to serve as an explanation why we did not
rid ourselves of her.

Kraus had taken Irma out of her unknown existence and
created a whole new background for her. I do not know exactly
how it was between her and the great iconoclast in the
beginning, although I should know, because the girl gave me
detailed descriptions of orgiastic nights with him, of which she
was not a little proud. Irma, however, had a fantastic
imagination, and lies leaped out of her mouth like red mice out
of the mouths of witches when they dance with Satan on the
Blocksberg. When I first met her, Kraus was still pretending to
be enraptured with the girl's divine beauty, but he could not
stand her chattering, and therefore introduced her to more and
more men who were supposed to take her out. It was not his
fault, I suppose, if a considerable percentage of these beaus
'knew' Irma after rushing her through the nightclubs.

Irma did not, of course, wait for Kraus to start her Messalina
existence, but she learned from him and his disciples to be proud
of her debaucheries.[12] She could not understand all the
philosophical talk and praise of the hetaera with which *The Torch*
overflowed, but she quickly realized that all she had
clandestinely practised from early puberty on, to the deep
dismay of her petty-bourgeois family, was now supposed to
represent the sublimest peak a girl could reach. When she took
sick in the course of her orgiastic life, she was celebrated as a
heroine honourably hurt in her struggle for love.[13] She could

scarcely read and write, but this, too, became something of which to boast in an era which sent women to colleges and into the arms of a neurotic emancipation. Women's emancipation was a matter of indifference to Irma, but she understood that she, as a great hetaera, was entitled to look down with contempt upon educated women. Looking down is a figure of speech; she was so petite that she could not actually do it.

No matter what one may say against Kraus, the nemesis of the *Neue Freie Presse* he had produced in the person of Irma his own individual nemesis, under whose weight he atoned for all his sins – his 'Privat Nemesiserl', to borrow a phrase from the old Viennese playwright, Johann Nestroy.[14] Nobody could bear her long, although she looked more than charming and compensated her lovers in the night for a good deal of what she vexed them with in the daytime by her immeasurable stupidity, lack of tact and complete absence of faith. Men sooner or later withdrew, and she always came back to Kraus, her foster father, who could not exert the brutality to let her down. Did she not resemble his lost ideal whose portrait, a bas-relief, he kept over his desk? Moreover, he felt responsible for the course Irma pursued: he had implanted ideas of grandeur in a hussy from the outskirts of the city, uprooted her and forced her to compete with downtown whores, much more gifted than she, with the result that she could not find her way alone any more.[15] Finally the little simpleton became as fat as a stuffed goose, and about twenty-five years after the time of which I am speaking, she died a suicide.[16]

★

When I entered the circle of Kraus's friends, however, Irma was the great hetaera – chin held high and walking proud, and I fell in love with her at once. I saw in her an impersonation of the war of liberation, which I and Kraus, and – as I thought then – Freud, too, had started. Kraus was the reformer and I his learned counsellor, as Melanchthon to Luther, very much secularized. Irma was our laboratory. I told her once that when on my way to her I felt as though I were walking over fields of white narcissi; she, knowing the cobblestones of the city street, replied: 'Stupid, there are no narcissi on Rochus Strasse.' Kraus explained to me how right she was to say that. There was, it seemed, no place for poetry in sex; all this romantic ballyhoo was the product of hysteria. Of course, men understand and need poetry, but women do not; beware of those who do. Some

23. The Hetaera of Lucian: illustration by Gustav Klimt from the German edition of *Conversations of the Courtesans*.

part of these distorting tirades was always true. Dante's Beatrice profited little from her lover's immortal poems. She almost never saw him; he loved her in her absence. The object of love poems is frequently absent even at the moment the romantic lover recites his products to her. He has his ideal within and projects it upon her. Many girls resent such a procedure, even if not quite aware of what makes them feel ill at ease when set in song. One can well imagine the dark lady's anger at Shakespeare increasing with his one hundred and twenty odd sonnets until she finally dismissed him with a curt: 'Oh, leave me alone, stupid!'

Another experiment: when lips come close to lips and a kiss was imminent logically as well as emotionally, Irma withdrew with a stereotypical smile. This, quite endearing in the beginning, became a bore, because she repeated it until no sense remained in the procrastinating gesture. Kraus said this reminded him of the hetaera of Lucian, the ancient writer who spoke of little lambs in green pastures, most animalistic and untrammelled, primitive, instinctual. I later nourished the suspicion that it was he who talked the girl into these preciosities, and that this explained her rigid adherence to them. Sometimes – and this probably came from him too – when ready to go out, to the theatre, for example, with hat and coat on, all of a sudden she looked at you with glowing desire, and you had to go back with her. Afterwards she used to say with a radiant voice: 'None of those bourgeois cows would do anything of the kind!' – a quotation from Kraus.

It was all marvellous, although tiresome, and the theory of it is all published: by Kraus and myself. The great poet and playwright, Frank Wedekind, came to Vienna and sat at our table.[17] In two plays, *Earth Spirit* and *Pandora's Box*, he had created the figure of Lulu, also a child woman, most attractive, stupid, animalistic and a good deal more sadistic than Irma, our more or less artificial child woman. Anyway, we had discovered the 'primeval woman' and her unlimited sex power. Again I feel like quoting Karl Hauer, a member of our round table who never smiled and spoke very little. He said to me, of course in the absence of Kraus: 'Oversexed! Genius of the pelvis! Beat it. This creature has no sex urge left at all, not for five cents. She is so desperate that she exaggerates lamentably.' This was cold water, but it did not cool my inspiration.

By nature Kraus was an ascetic who denied himself almost all the pleasures of life and did so increasingly as the years advanced. He praised the uninhibited and glamorous woman who gave herself to any man at any time without discrimination. He himself, however, did not wish to be one of these anonymous men; he wrote the prescription, let others swallow his pills. What he liked best (and this was his perversion, well known in Vienna) was to press the hand of such a female of whom he knew secretly that she was still panting from the embraces of her lover. In his theory he went further than anybody else. According to him, it was not only the right but it was the duty of woman to surrender to everybody whose appeal she felt. He denounced all women who could not do so as hysterical products of a sad era which was unproductive because the women were forced into a moral code which ran counter to their very nature. The spirit of the ancient hetaera was conjured

Wien, 29. Mai 1905

Einleitende Vorlesung von Karl Kraus

Hierauf:

DIE BÜCHSE DER PANDORA

Tragödie in drei Aufzügen von Frank Wedekind.

Regie: Albert Heine.

Lulu	Tilly Newes
Alwa Schön	O. D. Potthof
Rodrigo Quast, Athlet	Alexander Rottmann
Schigolch	Albert Heine
Alfred Hugenberg, Zögling einer Korrektions-anstalt	Tony Schwanau
Die Gräfin Geschwitz	Adele Sandrock
Marquis Casti-Piani	Anton Edthofer
Bankier Puntschu	Gustav d'Olbert
Journalist Heilmann	Wilhelm Appelt
Magelone	Adele Nova
Kadéga di Santa Croce, ihre Tochter	Iduschka Orloff
Bianetta Gazil	Dolores Stadlon
Ludmilla Steinherz	Claire Sitty
Bob, Groom	Irma Karczewska
Ein Polizeikommissär	Egon Fridell
Herr Hunidey	Ludwig Ströb
Kungu Poti, kaiserlicher Prinz von Uahubee	Karl Kraus
Dr. Hilti, Privatdozent	Arnold Korff
Jack	Frank Wedekind

Der erste Akt spielt in Deutschland, der zweite in Paris, der dritte in London.

Die Vorstellung findet vor geladenem Publikum statt.

Anfang präzise 1/28 Uhr.

24. Cast list for Kraus's production of Wedekind's *Pandora's Box*, 29 May 1905, with Irma Karczewska in the role of Bob, the groom.

up, uninhibited girls were called Greeks born too late in the midst of a Christian ascetic era which hunted them instead of worshipping them. His friends, Viennese epicureans, who saw the gap between this man's real nature and his fiery words, let him talk. I remember the reticent and sagacious Karl Hauer (may God have mercy on his soul!), who sat around listening in the coffee-house and told me one day, at a time when I was completely taken in by the spell of *The Torch*: 'I wish you'd stop that talk of Christian asceticism. There is no asceticism except in *The Torch*. Can you ever have a good time with Kraus? His idea of a good time is to call the waiter names because the soup is cold.'

Kraus, a man who had to be aggressive in whatever he undertook, debased women deeply while pretending that he fought for their sexual liberty and elevated them. It may be that Helen of Troy, Cleopatra (but not Shakespeare's Grande Amoureuse), Messalina, Lucretia Borgia, Manon Lescaut, resembled the type he saw. There were, however, Isolde, Juliet, Heloïse, to mention other great lovers, and there were Madame Curie, Florence Nightingale, Selma Lagerlöf, and so many more who certainly did not belong to the hysterical and unproductive type. Later I came to know this well, but for two years Kraus held me spellbound. One has to recall that we were really deeply buried in green-sickness, sexual inhibitions and hypocrisy. A sexual revolution was attempted in many places those days and *à la guerre comme à la guerre*. It seems to be a historical law that always before social revolutions, we see sexual revolutions at work. We were too much entangled in bourgeois prejudices, lived too far away from the soot of factory chimneys and the sweat of the workers to understand their cause. Hence we gathered under the flag of Kraus and there we fought for sexual liberty, winning a few victories which even today have not yet become common property.

6

The Rupture

The depression experienced during the trip to Venice did not subside in Vienna, although Kraus explained to me again that I was on the way to becoming a famous writer. I continued to write for *The Torch*, fighting for the liberation of human sex life. Once Kraus let me write an issue of the magazine all by myself in order to show me his high esteem. I filled this issue with an essay on syphilis. I emphasized that we were powerless against this disease as long as the puritanism of our ruling classes needed the venereal diseases as a bulwark for their morals. The old struggle between Christianity and paganism could be exemplified by this view of the plague. Our puritanical philosophy of life and the disease in question formed, I said, a vicious circle. I quoted Kraus, who in one of his most provocative aphorisms thundered: 'As Sancho Panza rides behind Don Quixote, so syphilis behind Christianity.'[1]

On 1 January 1908 I left the General Hospital, where I really no longer belonged, and opened a private office in the centre of the city. At that time it seemed to me a good idea to have an office on the Graben, the square in the centre of town adjoining St Stephen's Cathedral. I chose the hundred-year-old house, number 13, known locally as the 'Eisgrubelhaus' (little ice pit). The Graben, together with the Kärntnerstraße, form the main promenade of Vienna. I calculated that of the two hundred thousand people who passed by the place each day, at least one or two might drop into my office. But I was mistaken. I waited for patients in my little ice pit for over a year, and only two came. One was an epileptic who had a seizure in his place of business, which was next to my office. The other was a maid who, following an abortion, had a haemorrhage in the middle of the night. I must admit that I also had two patients by recommendation via the coffee-houses. One was an exceedingly

25. Turn-of-the-century photograph of the Graben in Vienna, where the newly qualified Wittels opened his consulting room.

affluent actress who suffered from constipation. I had to resort to abdominal massages, which I hated because the actress insisted on having them as early as eight in the morning. Moreover, she disliked paying me, saying: 'What would become of us if we started spending money so early in the morning!'

In order to equip my office I needed cash. Loan societies existed all over the country, and I chose one from Graz, capital of Styria, where every second man has a goitre. There is a deficiency of iodine in their water and for that reason the electrons in their brains revolve in slow motion. I needed two or three guarantors for the loan. Rich people do not readily sponsor one because, as the saying goes, their lawyer advises them against it. Poor people on the other hand are poor guarantors. I did not entertain much hope of obtaining that loan, until one day a man showed up in a Styrian hat with a green band and a goat's beard on it and introduced himself to me as the investigator for the Graz Loan Society. To make a short story shorter: I got two thousand Kronen from Graz, minus the two hundred which was Mr Schucklgruber's rake-off for attesting to his fellow Styrians as to my unimpeachable integrity.

Thus having suddenly become a man of means, I rented two

rooms and a foyer in the historic spot mentioned above. I furnished them as a waiting room and a doctor's office and slept on the couch in the office. This was the beginning of a beautiful time. I would have my private barber, Herr Clappwood, call early in the morning and shave me while I was still in bed half asleep. He was a philosopher and believed in 'early to rise'. 'It is so lovely outside,' he used to say. 'Even the street-car tracks are shining and the birds would chirp if there were any left in the city.' His was a losing plea, because the gentlemen of the nightly coffee-houses tugged in the opposite direction. I would rise late – no patients, no obligations – and when I walked out into the street I could feel that I was in the very heart of the city. This gave me a sense of happiness, renewed every morning, or rather early noon. I would cross the street and seat myself in the Graben Café, where Vincent the head waiter knew me well but liked me little. I paid with cheques on my new account. Vincent would have to give me change, which involved dispatching a boy to the bank with my cheque. Honest people generally pay in cash in Vienna, particularly when the amount is merely a few cents. Still, Vincent was a gentleman and never uttered a word of protest. After breakfast I would read the papers and then return home, crossing the street again and feeling happy once more to find myself in the centre of the city, rain or shine.

The reader may wonder how under these circumstances I earned my living. At first there was the loan, of course, and later I depended on my pen to support me. Had I not written and published articles and essays until my fingers hurt, I would have died of starvation – if I am permitted to exaggerate a little. Later it became clear to me why I moved out of the General Hospital and directly into the city centre. I wanted to live at the heart of the district where the coffee-houses and restaurants of our clique were situated. Kraus's company and the intellectual stimulation that came from him and his friends meant more to me than building up a medical practice for a livelihood. At long last I was in a position to get up late, breakfast in a coffee-house and see until late every night the people who sat in judgement upon cultural Vienna. I lived for a while what Kraus called an 'intelligent life'.

★

When I said that I had no patients, I really meant patients who paid in cash.[2] I did have many patients who paid in gratitude. The most illustrious of these was the architect Adolf Loos, who

26.   The architect Adolf Loos, one of Wittels's few patients.

had lived in America for some time and returned a changed man
– anti-Viennese, anti-baroque, anti everything old and established. He was hard of hearing, which made him increasingly
truculent. Lanky and gaunt himself, he would insist that the

Viennese would remain incapable of imbibing modern ideas so long as they continue filling themselves with heavy desserts, starched foods and the treacherous *Marillenknödel* (hot potato dumplings filled with apricots and covered generously with fried cracker crumbs).

His life in Vienna at the turn of the century was a complete revelation. Loos despised ornaments and religiously consecrated himself to their elimination. To the Greeks, Egyptians and Assyrians, he averred, ornaments really meant something. Our ornaments, on the other hand, are meaningless. He championed the vogue for smooth walls, inside and out, and simple lines in furniture. As for materials, rare woods, glistening metals, these had to be genuine – not *ersatz*. Instead of old-fashioned chandeliers, he would let the electric bulbs hang down on insulated wires. Objects of everyday use such as forks, spoons, dishes, he would preach, are not within the province of art. These had to be utilitarian products made by craftsmen and not the 'creations' of artists. 'Artisans never spoil anything,' he would say. A chair must be made by a cabinet-maker, not executed by Professsor Hoffmann. This last-mentioned gentleman entertained decidedly opposite views and was the advocate of art in everyday life, in contradistinction to Loos's asceticism. Hoffmann was the founder of the Vienna Workshop, today internationally famous, which promoted new taste in the manufacture of small objects.

Loos was an ardent fighter and an ardent hater. It took little to infuriate him. Open salt cellars on a restaurant table were wont to make him wild as a tiger cat. Why, he would exclaim, the patrons dip their knives in them after cutting their messy roasts. They should at least supply salt spoons. With all this fuss it seemed to us that Loos himself could have shown better table manners. Kraus, who appreciated Loos's creativity, said to us: 'Of course Loos misses salt spoons. He needs them to scratch his ear.' One night, attired in my evening clothes, I wore a shirt with three pearl studs. Loos shouted: 'Go away with that Hoffmann shirt!' and broke into an endless diatribe about the criminal instincts of a man who impudently wore a shirt of this kind.

Loos was my patient, but I lost his sympathy through my own negligence. Early one morning he came to me, the shutters were closed and I was still in bed. He sat down next to me, pointed to his face and asked: 'What have I got here?' I felt drowsy and replied: 'I must get more sleep, I'll come to see you a little later.' I must have forgotten about the appointment and did not call to see him until late that evening. When I finally arrived he told me that he had already seen another doctor and that he had erysipelas, a serious disease to have on one's face. At that time he was married to a charming English dancer, one of his four wives.[3] She was a tiny woman with a short nose protruding over a long upper lip, and she raged at me. From that hour Loos was my enemy. Whenever I passed his café he would turn his back on me with a jerk. Whenever he saw something I had published he would say: 'What's the use of reading it – if he wrote it, it's worthless.'

That year, 1908, I also began my first psychoanalytic therapy with a patient sent to me by Professor Freud. The treatment, which lasted two years, proved successful, and I reported on it in great detail at Freud's Wednesday group.[4] I swam elatedly in the psychoanalytic current. I was one of the few who foresaw clearly the world 'craze' it was destined to become. Freud was fond of me and did everything in his power to make me realize how evil an influence Kraus was. I would not heed his admonitions. At that time Kraus, the dreaded critic who annihilated literary authorities in the pages of his *Torch*, said to me that I was the greatest living German author – second to himself only – and that nothing could hamper my march to glory.

I continued to throw my articles in the face of the bewildered bourgeois. One of my best articles dealt with female political assassins.[5] I proved, in the one-sided and unjust way in which I then flourished the shining blade of psychoanalysis, that women assassins mean love when they kill, since they have displaced their sexual urge into aggression. I introduced the biblical figure of Judith as ancestress of the type I wished to describe. After years of widowhood she bestirred herself, made herself attractive, charmed Holofernes and destroyed him. Then I tried to show through a long series of women assassins in history, Charlotte Corday and several Russian girls among them, that the mechanism, though disguised, was always the same. What a triumph it was for me when I discovered that Vera Sassulitsch, who shot the Russian executive Trepow in 1872, was especially dressed for her purpose from head to foot.[6] Hat, shoes, gloves, underwear were all brand new; she wore every thread of it for the first time. We are not told, I exclaimed triumphantly, that Brutus did anything of the kind. These women celebrate their murders as though they were weddings. When all is said, I continued, it is better to be shot by this kind of woman; to live with her is even more fatal. This was supposed to be a blow at

27. Vera Sassulitsch (Zasulich), Russian anarchist whose motives Wittels analysed in a paper delivered to the Vienna Psychoanalytic Society.

hysteria, in connection with which I had always emphasized that it was the one disease which makes the environment of the diseased suffer more than the patients themselves. I was then still writhing under the pranks of Irma, whom I thought to be the diametrical opposite of all hysterical types because she had no inhibitions. Something was wrong with my theory.

All would perhaps have ended better, had I been capable of permanently freeing Kraus from Irma. He wished to get rid of her in good grace and directed her to stay with me. One day I told him that I knew he wished me to marry Irma.[7] He denied this and added, furthermore, that he thought I should not marry at all. This was the cue for the exchange about marriage already mentioned above. 'Why should he not marry?' exclaimed long, pale Mr Janikowski from Poland. 'He is a perfectly normal man. He has got to marry.' To be called a normal man in this circle was almost the worst possible insult, but Kraus made no attempt to defend me against it. Irma judged me quite correctly as a man who apparently was more than fond of her, but who had very limited resources. Repeatedly, after an argument with Kraus, she came to me quite perturbed, with the terrible news that Kraus meant to break off his relationship with her, although 'that cannot possibly actually happen'. I had sufficient influence with the man to restore the customary relationship, but we began to resent each other without being aware of it. 'Don't you think,' he said to me one day, 'that she has a talent for the stage!' I did not think so; but with some influence we succeeded in getting her a theatrical job in Berlin. She left for Berlin but was back after a few weeks. It was not that she was fired so quickly, but it seems that she tried to play the great hetaera, grandiose and arrogant, in Berlin, and could not succeed without our help. And so she left Berlin and came back to her friends and admirers in the Austrian capital.

A clever lady once said to me: 'Your friendship with Kraus cannot last long; you resemble him too much.' I did not understand the statement. To me, it seemed that I was totally different. I was little interested in his fight against the *Neue Freie Presse*. He was compulsive and I was easygoing, he was the man of the sharp and pointed thrust while I was more temperate. In addition, my work was based on the findings of a budding psychoanalysis, which Kraus not only could not grasp but to which he became more and more inimical. He, like so many enemies of science, had an inkling that Freud's psychology could see through him and his aggression.

People never talked quite frankly to me about my relations with Kraus. Perhaps they felt that I was not to be trusted or that I would not understand anyway. There were enough hints, however. Freud said: 'I hope you see that Kraus will make you pay for everything he has given you – and with interest.' His words were a somewhat impatient reply to one of my remarks that I owed so much to Kraus. At another time Freud said: 'You owe him much less than you think.' What he really meant was that Kraus was bringing about the ruin of my future.

One evening Kraus related a dream of his to the round table. He did not believe in Freud's interpretation of dreams, yet he saw a bad omen in this dream, as I did too. He was sitting – he said – in the midst of his friends. I was among them, and all the

enemies whom he had crushed by making fools of them had to
march by. We burst into derisive laughter at each one as he
passed. But when Benedikt, the arch-enemy, passed by and all
the other friends pointed at him with jeers and sneers, I alone
separated from the circle, approached Benedikt and bowed
deeply. This was the dream. 'The worst is,' Kraus added, 'that
my dreams usually come true.' This one never did come true,
inasmuch as I never met the editor of the *Neue Freie Presse*, yet it
had a very important connotation for me. Knowing the language
of the dream, I understood that Kraus wished me to be with
his enemies whom he could assault. As a veteran teacher of
psychoanalysis, I cannot resist the temptation to say a few more
words about this dream. As I mentioned before, Kraus, who had
attacked Benedikt like a maniac for many years, had somewhere
a deep admiration for the newspaper for which this man stood.
The dream shows both sides of Kraus. The component of
admiration is projected upon me; I separate from him and
change into an admirer of the hated father.

In May 1908 my own father died. Freud never spoke a truer
word than when he said that the death of one's father is the most
important event in any man's life. One does not feel that at the
time it happens. My good father had withdrawn from my
education a long time before and was satisfied with playing a
modest part in my life. He loved me and I loved him and we
were not demonstrative to each other. But behind the father in
the flesh there is a titanic magic figure, and one feels uneasy after
the death of the father. The child in us asks the anxious question:
'Where is my father?' and looks for him in all those unto whom
he has bestowed father authority. I went first to Freud and let
him know that my father had died. He had so many 'sons' even
then – later he had them by the hundreds – that he had learned to
take these projections with tact and restraint. It is almost a
matter of indifference what such a father person says to an
orphan just deprived of his own father; the man in distress,
regressing temporarily to a childish phase, can hardly hear it.
Freud said this and that, which evidently did not penetrate,
and ended with the words: 'We will remain together and work
together.'

Had I been in my right senses, it would have been easy for me
to compensate for the magic loss of the father, as far as this is
possible. I had Freud, whose doctrines were gaining rapidly in
magnitude and importance and for whom the circle of outside
appreciation was ever widening. I was one of the first to

recognize the power of his findings. At the end of April 1908, only a few weeks before I came to him with the report of my father's death, I was present at the first psychoanalytic congress in Salzburg. Sunshine was everywhere, and Freud introduced me to his international friends as one of his most promising young followers. The famous psychiatrist Bleuler was present with his assistant C. G. Jung, not so well known as yet, but an ardent admirer of Freud, together with many more scientists from all over the world. One year later Freud was invited to America and two years later, in March 1910, at the second congress in Nuremberg, which I also attended, he founded his international society that was to spread net-like all over the globe – and still exists.

Since early in 1905 I have never ceased to be powerfully aware of the genius of this man. Freud was fond of me and saw me as a somewhat troublesome colt that would develop into something really valuable later on; he accepted me as a naughty boy. My way was clear – or should have been. After the death of my father I should have closed the long-drawn-out interlude with Kraus and entered the temple of science without reserve. It did not work out this way. True, I did work with Freud, but a good portion of my unsettled conflicts remained in Kraus's camp. My reaction was utterly unconscious, yet for a long time I was the victim of a repetition compulsion, re-enacting my father's death many times through the loss of all my 'fathers'. Without knowing the unconscious motivation, I persuaded my medical teachers, Kraus, and later Freud himself, to drop me. It was not until many years later when I myself was analysed that I understood this compulsion. Despite my cheerful mask I was very unhappy, as becomes a son of Vienna.

My personal relations with Kraus deteriorated from day to day. He still printed my contributions to *The Torch*, but at long intervals, and seemed to prefer my psychological short stories. My psychoanalytical articles fell into disfavour. He, too, began to feel that I was too much like him. He later said that I imitated his style; at first he was not aware of it, he said, and considered my writings particularly good because they were so like his own. This is possible, even probable, as all pupils begin by taking over their master's ways. One does not usually hold this against the younger creators. It so happened that my last contribution to *The Torch* was published on the very day my father died.[8] It was the story of the daughter of a medieval count to whom a page and a future knight paid court. The knight makes love to her while she is in a faint, and the young girl develops unconsciously an unmitigated hatred towards him. She indulges in various schemes to ruin him until he is finally sentenced to die by the executioner's axe. At the last moment she repents and confesses all, but the ending, whether happy or not, remains vague. It is a sinister study of Freudian mechanisms, and I believe it to be my best. This synopsis cannot convey the atmosphere and the involved psychology of the hysterical plot.

In the summer of 1908 I collected two volumes of my writings for publication. One of them, which I thought to be of lesser importance, contained my short stories, mostly historical vignettes of old Vienna, which had previously been printed in *The Torch, Simplicissimus* and other German magazines.[9] My concluding short story in this book satirized Karl Lueger, the popular mayor of Vienna.[10] He was the idol of Vienna's women, handsome and a bachelor. He was also a devout Catholic and defender of the Church. My story dealt with Athanasia, a girl from a wine-growing district near Vienna, who was anxious to wed but did not know how. The excellent wine absorbed almost the entire libido of the young men in the district. She resolves to go on a pilgrimage to Saint Lueger in Vienna. There in the hustle and bustle of the big city she gets lost, and a stranger with a black beard (or was it blue?), of whom she asks the direction to the City Hall, after cross-questioning her pretends that he is Lueger himself. In a situation *à la* Amphytrion she succumbs, and when the man leaves early in the morning he instructs her to meet him later at the City Hall. When Athanasia gets there, she is refused admission. She tells her story in full detail to doormen, valets and aldermen, and she is finally ushered into the august presence of Lueger. The mayor in his blond glory seems so beautiful to Athanasia that she shuts her eyes. He realizes what has happened to this innocent worshipper of his and orders one of his officials to marry her, in an atmosphere which is a mixture of the Oriental despot and Dante's Paradise.

Kraus denounced the story as unworthy of the author who had written the stories which he had previously praised. Yet it had the same legendary style as the others, and I could not see the difference. I consider the story frivolous but truly funny. The other person who disliked my story was Lueger himself, to whom it naturally seemed sacrilegious.

The second book, to which I gave the title *Sexual Misery* [*Die sexuelle Not*], contained my essays on the family, women, birth

28. Freud's holiday home in Berchtesgaden, where Wittels visited him in the summer of 1908.

control, venereal diseases and the psychology of children.[11] I asked Freud for permission to dedicate this book to him, as without him it could not have been written. He accepted my dedication but remarked immediately that Kraus would see an insult to him in this dedication and would take his revenge. I said stubbornly that I did not care.

Later that summer I visited Freud in his holiday home in Berchtesgaden, which was as lovely then as now but not so widely known. I found him seated at his desk, and before him lay the sheets of a longhand manuscript, 'Analysis of a Phobia in a Five-Year-Old Boy'.[12] He hardly ever corrected or crossed out a word; his writings fell completely finished on the paper. Remembering Berchtesgaden in 1908, I am a little ashamed of my behaviour. Freud said that this analysis of little Hans proved for the first time that his statements about the sexual development of children were true. Our little angels know much more about the facts of life, and before we tell them, than we presumed. There is also more passion and more fighting spirit in them than our education likes to see. Freud had come to these conclusions before he analysed the little boy, from his analyses of adults whom he had remember their childhood struggles. There was a wide difference, however, between conclusions so contrary to generally accepted beliefs and direct observation. I

am afraid that, when I was in Berchtesgaden, I was so involved
in my own problems that I did not ask many questions; and
Freud did not make much of his work, which was to become the
foundation for an entire reorganization of our concepts in child
psychology.

There are those who have called the dead giant arrogant and
have claimed that he held too high an opinion of his own
importance. He had a high opinion of himself, indeed – why
should a psychological genius be blind just there? But his own
regard for the value of his work was expressed less in words
than in an enhanced grave dignity of manner. Could he not have
said to me in Berchtesgaden: 'This manuscript will inaugurate a
new era in child psychology'? He said nothing of the kind,
not then and not ever. In a letter to me, written as late as 1925,
Freud said:

> I am nothing but an investigator who, because of a remarkable
> coincidence, has succeeded in making a particularly important
> discovery. My own merits in this success will be limited to the
> practice of a few qualities of character, not frequent, to be sure,
> such as independence and veracity.[13]

That, it seems to me, is modest enough.

I had come to his summer cottage to read to him the preface
to *Sexual Misery*. I did so, and afterwards he invited me to stay
for dinner, but I ran away. He had invited me several times
before and I, stupid as I was, never accepted. Some inner shyness
prevented me from ever becoming intimate with him. He was
not the man to run after anybody, and so our relations, even
before the break between us, did not grow to the warmth of
which they were capable.

From Berchtesgaden I went to Munich to meet my oldest
sister Toni, the classicist of the family, who was always full of
Schiller, Goethe and Grillparzer. From there I crossed the Alps
to Venice, in order to find out how this city looked without
Irma. It was remarkable how quiet Venice seemed without Irma.
My first visit to Venice – I can hardly believe it now – took place
in January 1901. I arrived with an older friend who had just
graduated from law school. The city, so sunny in summer, was
damp and foggy. There were almost no foreigners to sweeten
the gloom of the buildings, which despite their beauty are really
in ruins. The famous Campanile (bell tower) collapsed the
following summer. The structure was over a thousand years old,

quite an amazing age for a heavy brick tower built on wooden posts sunk in the mud. The inhabitants spoke reverently of the event, emphasizing that the tower died like a gentleman, crumbling down into itself without causing injury to anyone on the crowded square. My friend and I saw everything in Venice in 1901. We came to the unanimous conclusion that this was no place for an unattached man. When I returned to Venice several years later with Irma, I gave up this notion and made this known to my friend in Vienna in a long letter. When I arrived for the third time, it occurred to me that perhaps not all feminine substance is moulded in so tiresome a pattern as Irma. Since that date I have been in Venice frequently, and I know now that all women must be divided into two groups: those with whom one can travel to Italy and those with whom one must not.

I was last in Venice in 1934, when I had a few hours' time between trains. At the terminal I took the *vaporetto* to the Ponte di Rialto. On the little boat I saw the newly wed petty-bourgeois couple from Germany and the florid elderly gentleman pointing out the palaces of the Canale Grande for their benefit, prototypes of so many eager young couples and so many 'connoisseurs' who come seasonally to Venice. The Fondacho dei Tedeschi, main post office of the city, a building of the fourteenth century and still in use, stands at the Rialto. I walked in and asked whether there were any letters for me as I had done so long ago. There were none. After that I proceeded through the Merceria to San Marco and leaned against the pillar of the Tower of the Giants. Nothing changes in Venice. It was about ten o'clock of a summer evening, people flocked over the pavement, a most mediocre brass band played Verdi and Gounod, and it was almost thirty years after the events related here. I did not look up the Giacomuzzi. What if Kraus's spirit were seated there thinking out malicious tricks against the *Neue Freie Presse*?

But my story still unfolds way back in 1908. Alone in Venice, I met a few friends and we sent a telegram to Kraus who was again in Sorrento, stating that we expected him in Venice for the celebration of the Emperor Franz Joseph's birthday on 18 August. This was a joke because *The Torch* every year made fun of the publishing by the *Neue Freie Presse* of silly letters and patriotic speeches of all the Babbits in the country. This, indeed, reminds me of Mencken and his *American Mercury*.[14] Kraus answered that he could not come, but he arrived the next day just the same. He seemed to be in good spirits, but not with me. Irma was not mentioned. Kraus and I were plotting something against each other without knowing it yet. He had started to make fun of psychoanalysis in his magazine, and this galled me. I cannot be sure whether it was then or later that he wrote the aphorism: 'Psychoanalysis is the disease for which it pretends to be the cure.'[15] Similar remarks had even then appeared in *The Torch*. I suspected from the start that while his blows fell on psychoanalysis they were aimed at me. The aphorism quoted is unusually good, a polemical masterpiece which no opponent of our science ever forgets, when once he has heard it. Not all of his remarks were equally good, some of them were mean and silly. It became more and more of a trial to be with him. Sometimes I asked him directly why he had changed. He invariably denied any change in his friendship with me. But I had changed, he said. My recent articles could not stand comparison with my older ones; it was as though they had not been written by the same man. My short stories were published in the fall of 1908, two months before my *Sexual Misery*. I wrote a dedication on the fly-leaf: 'To my dear Karl Kraus of 1907'. He said: 'What does that mean? It sounds so feminine.'[16]

Finally the atmosphere became so thick that I felt a kind of obsession to break with Kraus. Had I not done so, he would have forestalled me. I wrote him a peculiar letter paraphrasing the Forum speech of Brutus after the assassination of Caesar: 'Because you are a great writer, I revere you. Because you were my friend I love you. But because you – and here a gap must remain in Brutus's speech –' (that is what I wrote!) 'I will come no more to the coffee-house.'[17]

This was the letter. It was a parody, certainly, but the unconscious defence against underground tendencies is so clear to anyone familiar with psychoanalysis that I hasten to add that, so many years later, I am well aware of them myself. But then, in 1908, these mechanisms were still largely unfamiliar, even among analysts. Moreover, I was deeply entangled in the situation and would not have accepted psychoanalytic enlightenment while I was dealing and suffering these blows from my instincts within. To begin with, it was clear that the letter was a hostile action! Brutus killed Caesar. I know today why I chose the peculiar writing of a Brutus speech. A few years afterwards I published an essay on Brutus, in which I tried to prove that Caesar's assassin was actually not only the chosen son of the dictator, but that his deed, although rationalized politically, was a typical Oedipus deed. After the death of my father I had to kill the father image, the task before me being to live without a father. The 'gap' in my letter was my blind spot; I did not know the deepest determinant of my letter. We must interpolate 'because you do not behave as a father', or 'as you can never substitute for my father'. A good deal less profoundly I could have written: 'As Irma is more important to you than I am.' Such a remark would have been feminine indeed, as Kraus, not entirely without justification, had read between the lines of my dedication to him.

Kraus pretended to be greatly surprised by my letter. I expected him to answer: 'Nonsense! We will remain friends; come back!' I knew neither myself nor him well enough. He did not answer at all, but veteran fighter that he was, utilized his strategic position for building up motives for my step which debased me. I had betrayed him, he said, and sold him to his enemies. Having discovered such misdeeds, he worked himself up to an even hotter anger against me or, rather, the anger which had been pent up in him before he now let loose. He was through with me, too, and I had forestalled him by perhaps a day or perhaps but half an hour.

Irma behaved admirably. I saw her in a restaurant, but she would not sit down with me. She said she had no time. When I asked her somewhat facetiously: 'Is this the way immortal love affairs end?', she replied 'Sure' and turned her back on me. Thus was I unceremoniously dismissed. She had become surprisingly unattractive to me, too. Without Kraus she had no value for me, just as I had no value for Kraus without her. My relations with her had necessarily to go the same way as my relations with him.

Kraus had been collecting critical observations about me for a long time. He was one of those who collect 'material' against people in order eventually to use it. Shortly after my break with him an issue of *The Torch* came out containing his revenge: over seventy aphorisms, with me as the target and not in any flattering way.[18] Some of these aphorisms were very good – he was a master of the poisoned point. Others were less good, and most of them could hardly be understood by anybody but myself. Nowhere did he mention my name; instead I was always called the 'imitator', or the 'parasite', a sponge which had sucked its fill from others, a mean conniver, a man who belonged to the *Neue Freie Presse*.[19]

The aphorisms as such did not hurt me much. He had actually inspired me with his ideas; but then I too had given much to him. The well from which my ideas sprang was undoubtedly deeper than anything Kraus knew, and the future has shown that after we separated Kraus could not long continue on his path of sexual revolution. His exaggerations led him to an impasse. He later said that his ideas on women could not possibly be right because I shared them. I would have been able to survive the blow of Kraus's fourteen pages of aphorisms directed against me, but not so easily the fact that he could drop me so quickly and so completely, that he meant in this way to kill me. Was this the man who once, when we were staying in the country, feared that I might not be used to the cold night air and came back to my room to close a window? The man who had called me the greatest German writer and the only one who understood women as he did? It was unimaginable and confused me for weeks.

I sat in a coffee-house alone, in a different part of the town, and tried to think.[20] All the friends of Kraus, his round table, deserted me. He easily persuaded them that I had acted ungratefully and badly, and there may have been truth in that. The conflict, however, was more deep-seated, where good and evil, right and wrong, have no voice. A young lady who revered Kraus, and who was seemingly well disposed towards me, too, said to me over the telephone: 'Listening to you, one begins to think that you are right. The best thing to do is . . .' She hesitated and I finished: 'Not listen to me?' At which, just as unceremoniously as Irma responded to a similar question, the young lady said 'Yes'.

When I told Freud about the rupture, he asked a question characteristic of his unswerving psychoanalytic spirit: 'How is he after severing personal relations? Does he come back or doesn't he? If he came back to others, he will become reconciled with you, too. Otherwise he won't.' Freud was alluding to the law of repetition compulsion. Kraus never came back. I admit that I did not make a return easy for him. I was, of course, not the only man whom Kraus had first befriended and then turned against. On the contrary, there were very few whose friendship he could hold, and these only if the relations were superficial. I am among good company: Franz Werfel, for example, became his friend a few years after me, but not for long, either. But the position that I had occupied in relation to Kraus was unique – or so it seemed to me.

There I sat in my office on the Graben behind an enormous desk. Adolf Loos, the architect, had pointed out to me that a patient sees his doctor's importance in the measurements of his desk. But no patients came. I had neglected my medical practice in a shameful way, or rather, as there was none to neglect, I had not cultivated any. Freud sent me a patient, a young painter, whom I analysed with good results. Otherwise I was free all day to think. My book, *Sexual Misery*, was published with a pointed dedication: 'To my Teacher, Sigmund Freud, in Veneration'. I took no pleasure in the book. Another issue of *The Torch* came out with a second ejaculation of wrath, not as copious as the first, but just as venomous. From that time on Kraus continued to attack me in every issue.[21] My name was never mentioned, and he insisted that no living person was intended when he formulated his diatribes; they were just concentrated wisdom and nobody had a right to feel hurt.

I finally resolved that I had to take my revenge on Kraus. That, I felt, I had to do first of all. Afterwards I would see to building up my medical career. I had been asked before why I never tried to write a novel instead of short stories, and for some time I was tempted to write a novel in the manner of *Don Quixote*, whose hero should be a man who read so many detective stories that he lost touch with reality. Devoting himself to the war against crime, he finds out that the more dangerous criminals never go to jail. He loses interest in killers and thieves and starts to fight social dangers: politicians, exploiters, reformers themselves, always learning anew that all of them were victims of environment and circumstance. He also fights sexual immorality and, although he was a veritable puritan in the beginning, by continued dialectical experience he happens upon the child woman, whom he soon perceives to be the noblest of them all, the only innocent creature in the midst of lewd hypocrites. When he sees that one cannot live with the child woman either, he lands in an asylum, but leaves it again – and how to end the story was not yet quite clear to me.

After my break with Kraus I decided to use the framework of my novel as a vehicle for ridiculing him as the editor of a magazine which, under the pretext of fighting graft and corruption, advertises only the vainglory of its editor. I intentionally overlooked all the positive qualities of the man, derided his overgrown vanity, described his narcissistic infidelity and debunked the technique of his aphorisms, which were seemingly produced on an assembly-belt system. His sexual philosophy was unmasked as an over-compensation for his ugliness. Unable to conquer honest women, he debased them all to prostitutes. His name, in the novel, was Benjamin Disgusting and his magazine was called *The Giant Snout*. There was also an Irma figure, most favourably depicted as the lovely and innocent victim of a cruel world not created for beauty. The figure represented in the flesh all I had previously published about her in my theoretical treatises. Hence she was uneducated and oversexed, and was hated by the very same men who pretended to love her. Contaminated and impregnated, she finally died of tubercular consumption. Similar figures have been portrayed before in literature. Our real Irma had escaped all these dangers and lived on in blooming health. Our trip to Venice together became an incident in my satirical novel, and people who knew Irma well could recognize some of her features in my book.

In this way my book had become a *roman à clef*, a novel with a key. There was much talk in Europe about the so-called *roman à clef*, for which no equivalent term seems to exist in English. There is no story, novel or play in which those who know the author and his environment well can fail to find resemblances with actual persons. Authors take their figures from what they have known and observed, and the dilemma between the necessity of doing this and the fear of possible damage to people who feel themselves exposed to the public eye cannot always be happily solved. Some of the greatest stories, among them *La Bohème* and *The Sorrows of Young Werther*, have hurt real people in this way. Third parties, not infrequently, wax more indignant about the alleged outrage then the exposed persons themselves. The young model of my novel was not a lady with a vulnerable reputation, but was of such disposition that she herself was actually proud of my 'immortalization' of her. Her interests were not damaged. On the other hand, my figure of Benjamin Disgusting was an insult from start to finish and had been created for no other purpose. There were, however, extenuating circumstances: the model of my villain was a dragon with a dreaded claw who was not only well capable of defending himself, but who had insulted me first with his aphorisms *à clef*.

My break with Kraus dislocated the original plan of the book, and it became much weaker than it would have been without this intercurrent event. I had in mind a satirical review not unlike Voltaire's *Candide*, although I was of course sensible of the inevitable inferiority of anything I could achieve compared with that enchanting masterpiece. My own lust for revenge, unfortunately, could not be sufficiently sublimated, and here lies the real guilt of the author. Most readers of a novel are not interested in the author's models, whom they do not know anyway. But they expect and are entitled to a good book.

One night, while hard at the work of writing this novel in which I flayed my former friend, a feeling of intense bitterness and revulsion came over me and, on impulse, I did something which I later completely forgot. This is what I did. I tore off a piece of the sheet on which I was writing and quickly scribbled a few lines to Kraus, in which I suggested that we should forget all the anger and misunderstanding which had grown up between us and renew our friendship. I no longer remember what the words I used were, but I must have said I was still fond of him and willing to resume the common literary feuds as well as our personal relations. A short time later, the tenth anniversary of the founding of *The Torch* came around, and again I wrote to him in a friendly tone. I still did not know Kraus well enough. He did not answer, but added my letters to the Brutus letter and added them both to the rest of the 'material' which he kept in a trunk that might have borne the superscription: 'You never can tell what the future may bring.' To me, my action seemed very human – even magnanimous. He, however, saw clearly that my actions doomed me as defenceless as far as he was concerned. I was in an ambivalent phase, and the world has a contemptuous attitude towards what is called hate–love or love–hate.

I finished my novel and was pretty well satisfied with it. It was a terrific blow against my enemy. I was by no means certain whether or not I should publish it, and in order to come to a decision on this, I showed my manuscript to several people whom I considered reliable. A few, however, told Kraus what kind of bombshell lay in my desk drawer. A young lady who made me believe that she was on my side asked me to let her have my manuscript for a few days, so that she might read it at leisure. I acceded to this request and, manuscript in hand, she ran to Kraus, who now had an opportunity to read his condemnation at first hand, and this more than a year before it was published. He and his staff had ample time to prepare a defence. It was years later that I learned of this act of treason; Kraus promised the lady secrecy and kept his promise for some time. My 'double-crossing' lady expressed no guilt over her perfidious role. She said she saw no other way to prevent me from taking an unwise step. Today, doubtless, she would say that she wanted to protect my neutrality.

Kraus tried first to prevent the publication of my novel. He pretended that he did not know what was in it and let it be known that a literary attack against himself meant little. He might perhaps occasionally retaliate with a reply in the same vein in print. If, however, what he had been told was true, namely that the book attempted the exposure of a young lady of his circle, then he would not hesitate to go to court in her name. Through the intermediary of a lawyer he let one of my close relatives, then chief psychiatrist at the German university in Prague, know that my social existence was in danger and that he, Kraus, was in a position to destroy me.[22] The same lawyer went to Freud, gave him to understand that Kraus was not favourably disposed to psychoanalysis anyway, and indicated that Freud might judge for himself how much the caustic wit of *The Torch* could injure this young and exposed science. Freud was shown my letters to Kraus, but he must have had reasons for not speaking to me of them then. He asked me only whether it was true that a lady was vilified in my book. This I denied.

Many whom I had considered my good friends suddenly turned from me. They had been told all kinds of stories about me. I was about to expose a lady. I had shown black ingratitude to a benefactor by going over to his enemies. My literary connections fell away. My manuscripts were not accepted because anyone who took my part was sure to be attacked in *The Torch*. Even my publisher, Egon Fleischel and Company in Berlin, wrote to me saying they had heard that in publishing my book they were exposing themselves to all kinds of dangers and asking me to reassure them. I did so as best I could.

Meanwhile I had moved out of the Graben office which I had so foolishly opened a year and a half before and accepted a position in a private hospital, the newly founded Vienna Cottage Sanatorium.[23] I intended to stay there only a year or two but, as it happened, I remained resident physician of this hospital for internal and nervous diseases for about fifteen years, interrupted by a four-year period of service in the First World War. It was in that hospital that I got a good deal of my experience in neurology and psychiatry.

Perhaps I would not have published my book at all had Kraus not continued to call me names – a shady journalist, a born henchman of the *Neue Freie Presse* – and this although I had practically given up all literature and published nothing new, either in the *Neue Freie Presse* or anywhere else. When he was told this, he said: 'Of course, I won't let him!' These comments passed back and forth through the coffee-houses, from him to me, from me to him, although we did not see each other. He arrogated to himself a magic power over me and my pen, which

29.   The Cottage Sanatorium in Vienna, where Wittels was employed as a junior doctor.

annoyed me the more as I began to feel that there was some truth in it. I could not produce unless the damned book was published first.

In those days of the spring of 1910 I saw Freud almost every day as I was assisting him in the treatment of a hospitalized patient. My book was printed and almost ready for publication, and Kraus's interventionists redoubled their efforts. One day Freud asked me point blank to let him read the printed manuscript. He read it within twenty-four hours brought it back and said to me: 'I shall summarize my verdict in one sentence. You lose nothing if you do not publish this book; you lose everything if you do. The novel is bad. There are a few good passages in it because the author could not completely deny himself – that is all. Moreover, you have not told me the truth: there is all kinds of gossip about a girl in it.'

I tried to persuade him of the justice of my cause, but he grew impatient and said: 'Never mind the woman. He was your friend. When a friendship is broken, regardless of the reason, one has to keep silent.' 'But he is a dragon,' I replied, 'and insults me constantly in public. Have I no right to . . .?' 'You have none,' he insisted with great seriousness. 'If one of you behaves like a pig, there is no excuse in that for the other one to behave likewise. You remember my friendship with F[liess]? He attacked me in print, slandered me in a pamphlet, but I kept silent because of our former friendship. It makes an awful impression if two former friends throw mud at each other.'

As far as I remember – and we will see later that my memory failed me in this – he did not mention the affectionate letters which I had sent Kraus after the break. He moved me, but did not convince me of the untenable nature of my position. Finally he grew angry and said: 'Psychoanalysis is more important than your silly controversies. Why should I allow it to be damaged by your inconsiderate book?' It was obvious that I had no right to endanger the psychoanalytic movement. I would think the matter over once more, I said, and postpone publication. I mentioned that the book was printed and the publisher would make me pay if I withdrew at this point. 'How much will it cost?' he asked. 'I will give you the money.' I did not, of course, accept his generous offer. It was not a question of money at all. But I could see from his offer how much it meant to him. He was excited and so was I. He was right, and so was I – it seemed to me then. In order to keep Freud and psychoanalysis out of the struggle, I let Kraus know that Freud had done all he could to prevent the publication of my book. Actually I postponed it until the fall – this was half a year – in order to show the enemy that Freud had influenced me. Freud admonished me repeatedly: 'You still owe me your decision!' Finally he added: 'You are impossible in my circle if you publish this book.'

These words settled the question and made me definitely decide to publish. I was much too obstinate to let anyone threaten me. It was clear to me that after such a threat I would never set foot in Freud's circle any more. What kind of a circle was this to turn me out, me, centre of the universe! I immediately resigned from the Psychoanalytical Society.[24] Alfred Adler, then Freud's *locum tenens* in the society, told me that the 'Old Man' sometimes showed an inclination towards unduly forcible measures. He suggested that I tell him my case and, if it were good, he and his friends would keep to my side even against Freud. I considered my case good but too complicated to permit of discussion with outsiders. Besides, I did not wish to involve anybody else in my difficulties, and I declined Adler's friendly offer.[25]

7

The Scandal

At long last, in the fall of 1910, my book came out under the title *Ezekiel the Alien* [*Ezechiel der Zugereiste*]. The name of the prophet Ezekiel was given to the detective who, as a foreigner, came to the city of Benjamin Disgusting, the editor, and of Mizerl, the child woman.[1] The book gave rise to a scandal in more than one respect. Many were indignant at the indiscretion – they would never expose a lady in public. Almost the only one who did not feel indignant was Irma herself. She came to me a few years later, when everything had blown over, and wrote a dedication to me in the very same book, which I still possess; she felt pleased and honoured by my immortalization of her suburban existence.

Kraus had prepared everything and, with his counsellor at law, waited in Berlin for the appearance of my book as Nelson waited for the French at Abukir Bay. They had decided to sue, not me, but the publisher in Berlin; the plaintiff was not Kraus but Irma. She did not know why she should sue me; she was proud of the publicity, but she was persuaded that the publicity would be even greater if she sued for an injunction. She was back from Sweden and divorced, and reproached Kraus with having lost me because of him. I was, she said, the only one who really understood her, and there was no doubt in her mind that I would have married her in the end had not Kraus forced her to snub me. All this she told me a few years later. In her deep Viennese idiom she said: 'I told him that I was still in love with you, but he said: "What a horrible lack of taste!"' When she came to me with this confession, unfortunately, she had become quite stout and it would have been as troublesome for her to squeeze herself between the trees of the Hellenic woods as a Bacchante with her Thyrsus.

My strategic position in Berlin was bad. I was the one who

30. Cover design for the first edition of Wittels's satirical novel, *Ezechiel der Zugereiste*, 1910.

had encroached upon a young lady's sexual honour, and Kraus stood boldly in Lohengrin's armour to defend it. He never tired of emphasizing the fact that while he himself was debased in my poor piece of work, this meant nothing to him compared with a slur upon the honour of an unprotected lady. It was imperative to act at once and to prohibit the sale of the book lest the world learn that the plaintiff, let us call her Olga Ortshekova, had been the victim of a venereal disease. I protested that I could not see how anybody could reach such a deduction from the fact that a figure in my novel seemed to suffer from a discharge. Besides, Miss Ortshekova had not died as did the figure in my novel, and, as far as I knew, she had no children whereas the figure of my creation had. I stressed the fact that my opponents were even then, by their loud protests, spreading abroad the knowledge that Miss Ortshekova had had the misfortune to fall victim to an infection of which I knew nothing and certainly would not talk if I did know. In order to keep this unpleasant communication from the world, there was only one thing to do: desist from this lawsuit at once. The newspaper publicity had already driven my unpretentious book to its fourth printing. Irma, the nominal plaintiff, never came to Berlin and was not examined as witness in Vienna either.[2] It did not occur to me to insist on this step, which would have ended the proceedings quickly. I was not sued myself, but the publishing firm had an old and drowsy attorney who, like the two owners of the distinguished firm, hated the scandal. The papers in Berlin were almost unanimously on the side of the man who defended feminine honour.

Kraus had two lawyers, Hineman and Roth, famous for their cunning.[3] They cross-examined me and covered me with ignominy whenever I opened my mouth. 'Have you talked with your friends about your trip to Venice with Miss Ortshevkova?' they asked. I answered that I did not remember, at which Mr Hineman, a red-faced, asthmatic man–about–town (God bless his soul!) said: 'You told the story to me, when I was in Vienna, exactly the way it is reported in your book.' This was probably true, and Irma, for whom the elderly attorney had enthusiastically fallen, was most likely present and saying with a sweet and flattering smile: 'Oh you, stop it!' I mentioned something of the kind, at which Hineman shouted in a fit of rage that this did not belong in the record. I replied that he need not excite himself, I would not tell his wife about our gay nights in Vienna. At this the judge reprimanded me.

Kraus was interrogated as the first witness. I was not

permitted to be present at his performance. Hence I had to pass
up and down for almost two hours in the lobby of the
courthouse, unable to retire, because I had to be ready for my
call any minute. Then came the lunch recess. I saw my
publishers, who had heard Kraus's testimony and were quite
taken in by his eloquence. He fascinated them as he had me not
so long before. Kraus knew what I would say and forestalled
me. He told the court how I, an unknown young man, had sent
him essays which, while repelling him somewhat from the
moral side, showed talents which I did not really possess, as he
found out later. He could not detect this absence of talent right
away because I imitated his own style, which he naturally
considered very good. In order to improve my morals, a task
which, alas, later proved to be impossible, he invited me, a
seemingly gifted young man, to personal intercourse and this
gave me the opportunity of stealing many of his ideas. From the
start I showed no understanding of his fight against newspaper
corruption. His fight for emancipation of women, however, I
initiated with vigour. It was he who showed me that there are
women who show the essence of femininity on the surface,
while civilization as a rule forces women to keep this essence
deeply buried within them. This essence was love, and while
these women – here he enumerated the gleaming names of
literary figures in novels and plays from hoary antiquity to the
current season – were a danger to society and family life, one
had to protect them, innocent and attractive as most of them
were, against injury. It is because of the attibutes of their beauty,
shooting forth so early in life, that bourgeois society persecutes
them. But where would man be without beauty? From here the
treatise led into hysteria, touched upon asceticism, and dwelt
with profundity upon the hatred of the ugly for the beautiful, of
the weak for the strong.

    After I had behaved as though I understood these concepts,
the witness continued, I began to turn Kraus's struggle into
trivial and superficial oratory, and once he saw my inner
coarseness he had to drop me. At that time, however, I was so
infatuated with him that I could not accept his natural reaction.
Instead of leaving him alone, after he had made it quite clear to
me that he was through with me, I exposed a young lady in the
most shameful way, in order to hurt him. He wished to decline
to speak about the stupid insults against his own person;
anybody who knew him also knew that such things were
beneath his notice. But the honour of women – and Kraus could
thunder like a 'ham' of the old school – was dear to his heart,

and he would defend at any cost the woman who perhaps even then was crying into her pillow.

The atmosphere of the court turned against me. The judge, actually an examining magistrate, since the case never formally came to trial, was impressed by Kraus's resounding periods, the enchanting words of which were largely taken verbatim from my own articles published in *The Torch*. When it came time for me to give my own testimony, my plight was desperate indeed. Not having been present during Kraus's testimony, I did not know what he had said, and when my chance to defend my novel came at last, I used the very same tirades. He had told the judge that I was his imitator, and I myself proved by my own words that he had told the truth. Kraus, now present in the courtroom, interfered with my testimony by interrupting my sentences and ending them in a sneering way. He was reprimanded for this by the judge, but mildly and respectfully. When I had finished, stout Hineman pulled my two notes from his briefcase and asked me if I had written them. My hate–love was thus proved, and my cause in a bad way. 'Even his own teacher,' Hineman said aloud, 'Sigmund Freud has turned against him!'

The judge adjourned the proceedings in order to give both parties a chance to settle the case and my publishers asked me whether I really believed, as I repeated, that the suit would collapse if the court could see the plaintiff in person. I insisted on that, and the publishers suggested yielding in Berlin and having me republish my book in Vienna. Otherwise the legal process might drag on for a long time, for years perhaps. Kraus was well-to-do while I had no means and could get only an annual vacation from my new hospital in Vienna. So I accepted. Kraus won his action against my publisher in Berlin and my book, after four printings there, was republished in Vienna, where everything turned out as I had predicted.[4] Irma did not sue again in Vienna. Her lawyers probably dissuaded her from it, the sensation faded away and my book was more or less forgotten.

My relations with Freud were severed, and I did not see him for a number of years. The First World War kept me absent from Vienna for almost five years. We continued, however, to correspond. Whatever the occasion of my letters, scientific communications or the exchange of books we had published, I never failed to finish by emphasizing that he had done me wrong.[5] To this he always replied that, while he was still sorry he had lost me, he could not see that he had done me an injustice. After such a reply I said no more for a while until the glamour of the man made me write again.

In 1923 I felt that I wanted to describe to him in detail the circumstances of our break in order to force him to a more outspoken reconsideration of the old story. I said that I had first thought of making it part of my biography of him, which had been published earlier in the same year, but that I had ultimately changed my mind; the event was too personal. Freud answered with the following letter, which I have translated verbatim from his German:[6]

Vienna IX, Berggasse, 24 December 1923

Dear Doctor,
You were very right not to insert in your book the chapter which you sent me. It belongs to a different continuity. Reading it refreshed my memory of those events. Of course I cannot recall all I am supposed to have said or done, but I do not doubt in the least that your presentation is correct. One point, though, astonished me. Could it be possible that you have so completely forgotten the motive which was exclusively responsible for the severance of our relations and am I permitted to remind you of it? It is true that the 'scandal' with which the other side threatened was very unpleasant to me and that I would have sacrificed much to prevent. But certainly not you, personally, whom I appreciated. To that I was compelled only when the lawyer told me that you had addressed a certain person with affectionate letters while you were occupied with writing your lampoon. I do not remember any more whether he showed me these letters or only promised to do so, but my memory cannot fail me in the fact that when I asked you, you yourself did not deny these letters and claimed the right of acting that inconsistently because your feelings were ambivalent. Your insisting on this point, mixing up the real and analytical worlds, your refusal to correct this mistake, this was the thing that startled me in those days. I always considered Kraus's influence on you very disadvantageous and thought then that you had succumbed to it for good and were prejudiced for ever. On this point your recent communication has reassured me; but you will admit that a presentation of your affaire, omitting this point, would have been unfair; on the other hand it is impossible to mention it.
    With cordial greetings and best Christmas wishes,

Yours, Freud

PROF. DR. FREUD

WIEN IX., BERGGASSE 19

24. XII. 23.

Geehrter Herr Doktor,

Sie haben offenbar recht getan, dass
Kapitel, das Sie mir zugeschickt haben,
nicht Ihrem Buche einzufügen. Es gehört
doch in einen anderen Zusammenhang. Während
der Lektüre desselben habe ich die Erinnerun-
gen an jene Vorgänge bei mir wieder belebt.
Ich kann mich natürlich nicht an alles be-
sinnen, was ich gesagt oder getan haben
soll, bezweifle aber durchaus nicht, dass
Ihre Darstellung zutreffend ist. Nur ein
Punkt hat meine Verwunderung erregt. Können
Sie jenes Moment so gründlich vergessen
haben, welches für die Lösung unserer Bezie-
hungen einzig ausschlaggebend war und darf
ich Sie daran mahnen? Es ist ganz richtig,
dass der von der Gegenseite angedrohte
"Skandal" mir sehr unangenehm war und dass
ich manches geopfert hatte, um ihn zu ver-
meiden. Aber gewiss nicht Ihre Person, die
mir wertvoll war. In diese Notwendigkeit wurde
ich erst versetzt, als mir der Advokat mit-
teilte, Sie hatten zur gleichen Zeit, während
Sie mit der Abfassung Ihrer Schmähschrift be-
schäftigt waren, sich mit zärtlich werbenden
Briefen an die nämliche Person gewendet. Ich
weiss nicht mehr, ob er mir diese Briefe
zeigte oder nur zu zeigen versprach, aber ich
kann mich nicht darüber täuschen, dass Sie
selbst, darüber befragt, diese Tatsache nicht
in Abrede stellten, sondern sich das Recht
zusprachen, so widerspruchsvoll zu handeln,
weil Ihr Gefühl ein ambivalentes sei. Ihre
Unbelehrbarkeit in diesem Punkte, die Ver-
wechslung der realen mit der analytischen
Welt, die Sie nicht gutmachen wollten, dies
war es, was mich damals an Ihnen erschreckt
hat. Ich hatte den Einfluss von Kraus immer
für einen sehr ungünstigen gehalten und
glaubte Sie damals ihm dauernd verfallen
und für immer geschädigt.

31. Facsimile of Freud's letter to Wittels, 24 December 1924, recalling the Irma 'scandal'.

When I read this letter, I underwent the emotional experience,
well known in psychoanalysis, of the return of a repressed
memory. As I said before, I had forgotten this detail of my case
which, according to Freud, was of paramount importance in the
turn of events. All I remembered were Freud's words that I had
no right to gird at a former friend, and I do not recall any
mention of my 'love letters' in my decisive conversation with
Freud. Moreover, I still cannot see that my letters to Kraus were
a particularly unforgivable act. I can see that my behaviour was –
in the words of a clever Frenchman – 'worse than a sin – it was
stupid'. I was temporarily weakened by the death of my father
and by the strange triangular world in which I then lived.

Let us pause at this point to consider for a moment the well-
known psychoanalytic term 'ambivalence'. By ambivalence is
meant the almost simultaneous expression of two contradictory
feelings: love and hate, hope and fear, and – in general – assent
and denial. Such a condition is most undesirable in social life,
but it forces its way through to the surface whenever emotions

grow strong. Brutus killed Caesar, whom he loved, and then rationalized his ambivalent behaviour in an ice-cold speech wherein he declared that he had loved Caesar for certain reasons but had had to kill him for other reasons. Othello strangled Desdemona, whom he loved, because he had to hate her for alleged infidelity. Don José, in Bizet's *Carmen*, stabbed his adored idol to death when about to lose her to another man. I, too, turned against my former friend because I could be his friend no longer, or perhaps because he could not continue cordial relations with me. When I was on the point of punishing him in the equivalent of a duel of writers, I felt impelled to make an attempt to do better than that and wrote to him affectionately. Let us suppose that Kraus had been a different man and had accepted my offer; all might have turned out well. We could not, I can see that now, have gone on – too much paranoia had crept into our relations, on his side as well as on mine. But the trouble arose exclusively from my opponent's use of my letters in public. His hatred of me made him react in a way most strange and unfair for a writer who had ample opportunity to match literary offence with the same weapons.

I can see that under the circumstances Freud had to drop me. He saw the incipient scandal, some part of which would inevitably attach itself to the psychoanalytic movement: one of Freud's pupils involved in an act of indiscretion, obnoxious theories on sexuality publicly discussed, psychoanalysis stigmatized in the person of one of its foremost exponents. Freud, in his letter to me, repudiated this point of view as the decisive one in the severance of our relations. Yet there was sufficient justification in the practical situation for the leader of a worldwide movement to separate from me at least temporarily until the matter had become a thing of the past. There is, however, this one element which I never understood and still cannot accept: why my so-called 'love letters' to Kraus, which in the event of success would naturally have stopped my 'lampoon' and become meaningless, should brand me, because they were not successful, as an unbearably ambivalent man who refused to correct a most obnoxious mistake. We will have to return to this point later.

Freud and I might have perhaps found our way back to one another earlier, had it not been for the intervention of so many things beyond our control. Before the outbreak of the First World War in Europe, we were angry at one another. I was of the opinion that he had let me down in one of the gravest crises

32. Certificate awarding Wittels a medal for bravery during the First World War, 26 July 1916.

of my life, and he was angered that he had cause to reproach me. It is clear that the leader of a young movement, and one so bitterly contested at every step, could not possibly allow me to cut such capers. On the other hand, wrong though I may be, I feel that I might have submitted with grace to his wishes had he proceeded in a different way. He was inexorable, I was obstinate, and the clash was sharp.

With the year 1914 came the war, and Freud saw his three sons called to the colours. I myself was absent from the city of Vienna for almost five years, first on the Polish-Russian front, later behind the Italian front and finally, for three years, in Turkey, Syria and Mesopotamia. In the brief period between the inglorious conclusion of my interlude with Kraus and the outbreak of the war, Freud had his hands full with the defections that befell him between 1912 and 1914. There was Alfred Adler, whose new psychology, based on the concepts of inferiority and aggression, grew mushroom-like and seized the public eye.

Then came C. G. Jung, with whom Freud was forced to break because of Jung's marked deviations in matters pertaining to the libido theory. Both dissenters had their adherents and founded schools of their own, and this grieved Freud, as he himself has said in his essay 'On the History of the Psychoanalytic Movement' (1914) and as I later reported in my biography of him. Shortly afterwards Wilhelm Stekel was forced to sever relations with Freud for personal reasons, which were only superficially masked by scientific differences. These new antagonists were more dangerous than outright enemies of psychoanalysis, who as a rule knew little about the subject they decried. Speedy defence against all these opponents was needed, and Freud, assailed by the pack, stood his ground, defending himself with vigorous blows. These scientific feuds have been reported in detail elsewhere; let it suffice to recognize that they were to go on for years. The spirit of the times was not conciliatory.

Within the span of three years I published as many books; first a small volume, *Tragic Motives*, then a larger one, *All for Love*, and finally a psychological novel, *The Jeweller of Bagdad*.[7] When my *Tragic Motives* came out in 1911, Freud was still so angry at me that he refused to read the book. Later he wrote me that he had heard that it was a good psychoanalytical study and would like me to send him a copy, selecting for myself in return one of his books. I had copies of all his books, of course, but I asked him for a copy of his *Theory of Sexuality*. My little book was applied psychoanalysis, a new understanding of the meaning of tragedy. Today it is fairly common to apply the concepts of psychoanalysis to non-medical phenomena. I was one of the first to indicate its value in the elucidation of the fields of sociology, literature, politics, pedagogy and criminology.

An ocean of ink has been spread over the problem. What is tragic? Instances of so-called tragic death, such as occur in automobile accidents, in accidental falls from high places or even among the hundred thousand men killed in war, are not necessarily tragic. One single Ophelia losing her mind through unhappy love has made more tears flow than the statistically provable fact that the corpses of the world war laid end to end would span the equator several times. We demand of a tragedy specific qualities lacking in the ordinary accident. In these mixed feelings of pleasure and pain, our unconscious, as described by Freud, plays an important part. My contribution to an understanding of tragedy was that the cause of all tragic events is an irresistible intrusion of unconscious motives into the conscious and active mind. In our unconscious we harbour illogical, unethical, ambivalent impulses which the conscious stream rejects. We live in permanent danger of short-circuit between the systems conscious and unconscious. From this derives the possibility of tragic guilt. For example, Hamlet's unconscious incestuous love causes the destruction of Ophelia and himself, while Othello's jealousy is rooted in the feelings of inferiority of the Moor. My theory stimulated writers, philosophers and actors, and the subject has been seized upon and widely discussed since its publication thirty years ago. The book was little quoted, for I was taboo that year in the psychoanalytical journals, and the literary magazines had no use for my offerings either. I had fallen between two stools.

The second book of this period, *All For Love* (1912) was, in the main, the presentation of a fantastic vision of primal man. I opposed the generally accepted belief that human civilization originated from want, perhaps from the universal impoverishment overcoming the earth in the glacial periods. I tried to prove – as far as one can speak of proof in these matters – that man is a creature of abundance originating from the pre-glacial tertiary epoch. Man differs from mammals below him by a considerable advance of his *libido sexualis*. There are no more shortlived mating periods interrupted by long spans of sexual indifference, but permanent love of the sexes with a consequent deepening of the erotic life. Sexual habits were formed which were no longer subject exclusively to the principle of propagation, to which the animal kingdom is without exception subservient. An animal in dire need and hard pressed in the struggle for existence would have had no possibility of sexual overactivity. In short, therefore, primal man must have been a product of natural wealth, sunshine and song. Later, when with the glacial era a period of poverty set in, sufficient human, or rather pre-human love culture was built up which could be adapted to the new and hard conditions of life. Civilization is applied love culture.

This was the main idea of my primal world phantasia of 1912, which for the reasons mentioned above did not meet with much attention. In Freud's sense I showed that libido was the god Eros, the constructive principle expanding over everything that happens in the world of the living and above all in our civilization. People said, as they continue to say, that this is a one-sided exaggeration and 'sex' could not possibly be everything. When one tells them that the sun is the origin of all life and all warmth, they might say with the same lack of understanding that this is an exaggeration because we have coals and oils which give us heat, too. I hope some day to publish my phantasia in English. It is, I must admit, somewhat obscure, but so is the German forest in which it takes place. And yet the nebulous semi-darkness of the Teutonic forest is the loveliest retreat in that strange country.

8

Reconciliation

After the war I was occupied with social planning for more than a year. I never belonged to any political party, but worked for a plan similar to the one which, under the name of technocracy, grew suddenly in popular interest a few years ago in America and then subsided. My war experience had influenced me profoundly, and there were many like me in this.[1] We actually hoped that the veterans of all countries, those who emerged sane from the war, would unite and introduce an order of fraternity. This had not happened at the beginning of the war, as had been partly expected. The proletariat of all the countries did not then unite; they thrust their bayonets into one another's bellies instead. Nor did they unite after the war. We thought that the defeated countries at least would feel inclined to condemn war and, after their atrocious experiences, be amenable to a simple plan securing the fundamentals – food, shelter, clothing, care for the sick, a minimum of education – for all men. It took me one year to recognize that such a plan had no chance whatsoever. During the war the life of the individual was considered valueless, and there was no reason why this philosophy should change after the war. So we were mistaken. The generals, not military leaders alone but leaders in the fields of education, economy and politics, rendered all socialistic planning impossible for the time being.[2] Such plans are rightly called utopias. We psychoanalysts know a few things about the need and the difficulty of introducing fraternity and love into economics. There are, however, others who believe that fraternity can and must be shot into the masses with machineguns. They feel that a lot of shooting must be done first; fraternity will follow later. This they call their scientific conviction, but it is a conviction which some other people do not share. I ended my propaganda for a national working army to provide the 'minimum' for everybody with a book which I called *An End to Poverty*, published in England. I was not able to interest an American publisher in the idea, but Upton Sinclair took cognizance of it and used my title in the slogan *EPIC* in his campaign for governor of the State of California, *EPIC* meaning *End Poverty in California*.

After an interruption of about six years I returned to psychoanalysis. The man who helped me find my way back was Wilhelm Stekel, one of the oldest pupils of Freud, who, in 1912, two years after me, succumbed to the centrifugal forces around the master. Stekel died in England in the spring of 1940. Made wiser by my experience with Karl Kraus, taught to be silent about former friends, I will not talk here about Stekel's character, which is not always judged favourably. It is easier for me to say little about him because my relations with him were never as intimate as they were with Kraus. I had known Stekel since 1906, having met him first at Freud's round table, but I had little close personal contact with him then. In 1920, I met him again on the streets of Vienna. He told me, in his narcissistic way, of his great successes, his books, his patients, and his pupils. He also told me how Freud had injured him and how, despite his successes, he still suffered under this injustice. That was grist to my mill. There was little I had to tell Stekel because he was well informed about my rupture with Freud. The tempter rose again in my life: this time, however, in the form of one to whom I came to owe gratitude, although Freud later did not think so. It is my opinion that I would not have found my way back to psychoanalysis without the help of Stekel.

Stekel's was a peculiarly magic nature.[3] Without Freud's discovery Stekel would never have known that the dream spoke a language which could be understood. But once he was given the key he became a dream interpreter whose equal I have never seen. He could read the dreams of his patients as easily and readily as other people read books. Much of our knowledge of dream symbols came from him. He recognized the symbol of death in dreams. ('Every dream is a picture puzzle with the question: Where is death?') He knew that right and left meant right and wrong, described bisexual symbolism in dreams, found out that the figure five represented the hand, twelve the last hour, and divined the meaning of many more symbols in the picture language of the dream which had not yet been recognized by Freud. As easily as he saw through dreams, Stekel was aware of hidden aims and unconscious fears in listening to

33. Wilhelm Stekel as a young man.

his patients' communications. Stekel knew little of the so-called resistance analysis carefully elaborated by Freud's school, had not much use for systematic methods in general and was proud of it. Freud commented on Stekel's methods of practising analysis: 'We are told that savages put their ears to the ground and in this way are able to hear the tramping of horses for miles. Civilized man cannot do this, but he has the telephone and wire which send him messages from much greater distances; in other words, we have science and its methods.'

When analysing, Stekel was almost absent-minded and his strange ease in understanding reminded one of the accomplishments of mediums. He must have had some procedure, but we could recognize none to study, and as a teacher he was rather incoherent. A man with such qualities had to become an offence

34. Stekel towards the end of his career, holding a pet dog.

to scientists. He was like the mental arithmeticians who call out the results without using any observable method. Science, however, demands not only results but methodical evidence leading to the results as well. It is distrustful of magicians, and rightly so. Stekel was often wrong, too, and had a way of gliding over his mistakes with facility and without compunction. But here we would pass judgements on character, and these I have promised to avoid.

To me he spoke of the old days, of how I had come to the psychoanalytic round table as a young fighter and how, later, after my breach with Kraus, I had collapsed as though I were no longer the same conquering man. But I had to resume my destiny, he knew I would. He had his own school now, he said, and Freud's school was entangled in mysticism and philosophy while true analysis, the medical work, lay with Stekel. I knew little then about the latest events of the movement, and some of what he said seemed justified. I told him that I did not think it possible for me to find my way back to psychoanalysis without Freud. He contradicted me on this; it was, he said, quite simple. My psychoanalytic knowledge and talents were repressed because of defiance. I should go through an analysis which he was willing to carry out, and after this I would know more of the subject than any one of Freud's pupils. All my knowledge and understanding would again come to the fore. I followed his advice and I must confess that I had in this analysis most shaking experiences and I made discoveries which surprised me greatly, although I had practised analysis myself since 1908. Intellectually I had known all the mechanisms many years, but almost nobody is actually convinced of them until he has himself felt through analysis their blind and irresistible power.

Stekel's method was not to have any. Not always did I lie on a couch. He lived in a suburb where the city bordered on the woods, and sometimes in the night we walked over snowfields scantily lit by the last city lights and he analysed me while we slowly walked together side by side. The idea must be horrifying to any classical analyst, and I myself do not pretend that it was a method to be recommended. Whenever Stekel felt that he had something to say, he stopped. I stopped, too, and in a completely dispassionate voice, as though it were a matter to which he was utterly indifferent, he stated terrible facts, dug out the big shocks of life of which one had either known nothing before or whose importance to one was by no means clear. Stekel's beautiful police dog ran ahead of us, his cane in mouth and returned again and again without the cane. 'It is a valuable stick! A souvenir!' Stekel would exclaim, and my analysis was temporarily disrupted while the dog was made to seek for the cane in the snowdrifts. It was regularly found and as regularly brought back, after which the mysteries of our story slowly continued.

I have kept the impression, although my memory may be wrong, that my analysis in the snow yielded better results than on the couch. The trouble with Stekel's analysis was that it almost invariably reached an impasse when the so-called negative transference grew stronger. In this phase of the work patients become unruly and a special technique is to be used to enable the analyst to deal with this unpleasant but unavoidable and even helpful part of the work. Stekel was too narcissistic for that. He took criticism and reproaches from the patient as a

personal offence and cut the analysis short when, in the Freudian
sense, it was just about to begin, with the patient's frustrated
feelings coming to the fore. For this reason his analyses lasted a
relatively short time, and this was the point on which he prided
himself. He claimed that his was 'active therapy' as opposed to
the long 'orthodox' analyses which he derided. Inasmuch as the
negative transference, by the nature of psychoanalysis, comes
sooner or later to the surface, his analyses could not last long.
Here was one of his numerous inconsistencies. The fundamental
rule of psychoanalysis is that the patient must say whatever
comes to his mind. It is inconsistent first to pledge a man to spill
it all out and then, when in strict accordance with the rule he
does so and manifests aggression towards the analyst, to rebuke
him. Once a patient said to him: 'How long will I have to come
to you? I am sick and tired of it.' Stekel replied: 'You do not
have to come any more; your treatment is at an end.' He was
gravely offended that a patient could say such a thing to him
who was the great expert, interpreter and benefactor. Instead of
revealing the phenomenon of negative transference, he dismissed
the ungrateful neurotic.

This, however, did not always happen. If he liked his
'analysand' and if he hoped to win a partisan for the future (as in
my case), he took plenty and could treat negative transference,
too. It was quite clear to him that I felt superior to him in many
respects and had him analyse me only because I was too proud to
go back to Freud. He was particularly cautious with me and – I
gladly admit it – quite efficient. He said that Freud had treated
me the wrong way throughout. To him, Stekel, it would have
been easy to keep me from publishing *Ezekiel*; Freud could have
succeeded, too, were it not for the fact that he had been blind in
the matter since he had lost so many friends himself. We
discussed the crucial point of my sweet letters to Kraus after
Freud had recalled them to me, and Stekel said this was nothing
at all, hardly worth mentioning. In matters of ambivalence,
however, he was not trustworthy, and I did not accept his
judgement wholeheartedly.

Shortly after my analysis with Stekel was finished or it may
have been while it was still in progress, Mr E. P. Tal, a
publisher, called to ask me whether I would be willing to write a
survey of psychoanalysis understandable to the layman. He had
in mind more the general scope of Freud's work than the
medical aspect of psychoanalysis. He had first asked Stefan
Zweig, but Zweig had declined because, as he said, he did not

feel competent for the task. Tal asked him who, in his opinion, could write such a book, and Zweig answered that he did not know of anybody. When Tal mentioned my name, Zweig replied: 'Yes, I think he would be the man to do it.' I do not know whether Zweig remembers this conversation, but it was in this way that I was honoured with a commission to which I probably owe my present position in America.

In my analysis with Stekel there was, as one may imagine, much talk about my book *Ezekiel*. We discussed the entire episode with its roaring complexes, its shifting ambivalences and its nucleus in the father problem. To undertake, while in analysis, to write another book whose impetus lay in a personal relationship was certainly a dangerous enterprise, about which my analyst should have warned me. A book written under these circumstances was liable again to become ambivalent and aggressive, to represent psychoanalysis and its creator subjectively rather than with the desired objectivity. Kraus had been a bad father and I had punished him. Now Freud was a father, too, and a bad one in that he had rejected me.[4] Stekel buttressed my opinion that he was a bad father, and an argument never settled, never quite forgotten, was stirred up anew.

I did not know how to proceed at first. Stekel produced enormous volumes without interruption. They came out of his clattering typewriter with inconceivable ease. He could not understand what there was to think about. He said: 'Sit down and write!' I, however, realizing that I had reached another turning point in my life, spun myself deeply into psychoanalytic literature, Freud's publications in particular, for half a year. I knew all Freud's works well, anyhow; those of the first decade of the century I had discussed with Freud and our groups as they appeared one after the other. Those of the second decade I read as fast as they were published, as did all his pupils.

Delving anew into Freud's *Interpretation of Dreams* and other works, his *Psychopathology of Everyday Life* and 'History of the Psychoanalytic Movement' especially, I found that although he repeatedly said that the public had no right to pry into his private life, he had published so many details of his personal life that it was possible to construct a biography of the man and his work without further study and therefore without indiscretion. No authorization was necessary if I used but printed material with a few interpolations of my own. This was quite a discovery. Stekel had told me a few things about Alfred Adler and C. G. Jung which I had not known, and as both of us judged the defections of these two psychologists in much the same way that Freud himself did, no specific consultation with the master was needed in this matter either. The only sore point was Stekel himself. Freud could not bear the sight of him and missed no opportunity to point this out verbally or in writing. The real aim of my book was to show Freud that I, from my more distant position, knew him and psychoanalysis better than did the pupils by whom he was daily surrounded. It was a kind of *El Cid* ambition, inspired, perhaps, by the comment of the king during the banishment of the knight from the Spanish Court: 'Why, banished though he is, he serves me better than any one of you!' This, I hasten to add, though I knew it not at the time, was a piece of self-analysis which I perceived later on. I overplayed my hand; I was not as wonderful as I thought.

The style of the book was not uniform. Expressions of admiration and reverence alternated with hard, occasionally ironic, criticism. Freud's doctrines were presented in a readable form and not without inspiration. I later had to admit that the critical sections of the book were partly untenable; other parts (including my remarks on anxiety, on certain 'Freudian blunders', and on the concept of his book on dreams) I not only could support myself but saw accepted by Freud.

Again I had produced a mixture of ambivalent feelings and aims. On the one hand I wished to punish the bad father; on the other hand, as I see it now, I hoped to be welcomed back as the prodigal son. In addition, I was grateful to Stekel.[5] He had been of help to me, and I wished to help him in the public eye. It is strange to say that this book, with its manifold and seemingly incompatible aims, was a complete success. It is out of print today and I do not intend to prepare a new edition. It was published in German before the Christmas of 1923 and a year later in English and French. It made my name internationally known to those interested in Freud, regardless of whether they were for or against him. I was introduced, at uncounted lecture desks in Europe and America, as Freud's biographer; yet I was, as Freud later said, an 'unsolicited biographer'.

I had just finished my book when I learned, to my utter consternation, that Freud was very ill and had to be operated upon because of cancer of the maxilla bone. Had he died, my book would have become meaningless to me. It contained my settlement with the man whom I loved and admired. Long ago I had been 'naughty' and he had punished me. My biography was naughty again with the unspoken aim of being recalled to favour

SIGMUND FREUD

DER MANN
DIE LEHRE
DIE SCHULE

VON

F R I T Z   W I T T E L S

„Il faut admirer en bloc!"

1924
E. P. TAL & CO. VERLAG
LEIPZIG / WIEN / ZÜRICH

SIGMUND FREUD

*In unwandelbarer Verehrung,
in Erinnerung an Zeiten, die nun
schon lange vergangen sind*

Dr Fritz Wittels
Weihnachten 1923

35.   Title page of Wittels's biography of Freud, with handwritten dedication.

in spite of it or perhaps just because of it. I felt that I had been aggressive but brilliant. All depended on his reading my effusion. And then I learned that he was caught in the grip of a dangerous disease. My enemies assumed, on the contrary, that I had written my book with the purpose of being the first in the market after the man's death. He recovered, fortunately, and survived his first operation for sixteen years.

Around Christmas time in 1923 I sent my book to Freud, who received it with undisguised surprise. His first impression of the book was not unfavourable.[6] A few days after receiving my book he wrote me a letter, which I published one year later, with his authorization, in the English edition.[7] He also corrected a few matters of fact in my text, and these corrections I included in the English edition. His letter contained several scathing comments on Stekel, and I asked for permission to omit them in the publication which was then pending. He permitted the omission of one particularly offensive part; two others had to remain. My book is now out of print, and I repeat the letter here as it was published (in translation) in 1924, still omitting the strongest condemnation of Stekel but adding, however, another

passage which I had then suppressed for obvious reasons. Here it
is: 'Perhaps you know that I was seriously ill, and although I
have recovered there is still reason to see in my experience a
warning of a not too distant end. In this state of partial removal I
may be permitted to ask you to acquit me of the intention to
disturb your relation to Stekel. I am only sorry that it gained so
decisive an influence on your book about me.' And the letter:

> You have given me a Christmas present which is very largely
> occupied with my own personality. The failure to send a word
> of thanks for such a gift would be an act of rudeness only to be
> accounted for by very peculiar motives. Fortunately no such
> motives exist in this case. Your book is by no means hostile;
> it is not unduly indiscreet; and it manifests the serious interest
> in the topic which was to be anticipated in so able a writer
> as yourself.
>
> I need hardly say I neither expected nor desired the
> publication of such a book. It seems to me that the public has
> no concern with my personality and can learn nothing from an
> account of it, so long as my case (for manifold reasons) cannot
> be expounded without any reserves whatever. But you have
> thought otherwise. Your own detachment from me, which
> you deem an advantage, entails serious drawbacks none the
> less. You know too little of the object of study, and you have
> not been able to avoid the danger of straining the facts in your
> analytical endeavours. Moreover, I am inclined to think that
> your adoption of Stekel's standpoint, and the fact that you
> contemplate the object of study from his outlook, cannot but
> have impaired the accuracy of your discernment.
>
> In some respects, I think there are positive distortions, and I
> believe these to be the outcome of a preconceived notion of
> yours. You think that a great man must have such and such
> merits and defects, and must display certain extreme
> characteristics; and you hold that I belong to the category of
> great men. That is why you ascribe to me all sorts of qualities
> many of which are mutually conflicting. Much of general
> interest might be said anent this matter, but unfortunately
> your relationship to Stekel precludes further attempts on my
> part to clear up the misunderstanding.
>
> On the other hand, I am glad to acknowledge that your
> shrewdness has enabled you to detect many things which are
> well known to myself. For instance, you are right in inferring
> that I have often been compelled to make detours when

following my own path. You are right, too, in thinking that I have no further use for other people's ideas when they are presented at an inopportune moment. (Still, as regards the latter point, I think you might have defended me from the accusation that I am repudiating ideas when I am merely unable for the nonce to pass judgement on them or to elaborate them.) But I am delighted to find that you do me full justice in the matter of my relationship with Adler. . . .

I realize that you may have occasion to revise your text in view of a second edition. With an eye to this possibility, I enclose a list of suggested amendments. These are based on trustworthy data, and are quite independent of my own prepossessions. Some of them relate to matters of trifling importance, but some of them will perhaps lead you to reverse or modify certain inferences. The fact that I send you these corrections is a token that I value your work though I cannot wholly approve it.

It seems to me that no one who reads this letter can gain the impression that Freud felt deeply hurt by my book. On the contrary; Freud must have seen the glorification of his personality which I had in mind. The evident sincerity of the interspersed criticism, harsh though it sometimes was, enhanced the magnitude of the man and his work. Where the sunlight is strong, so to speak, the shadows lie deep. Of course one may say the very opposite: that criticism coming from a man who obviously valued him highly, condemned him. Readers adopted one or the other of these outlooks according to their attitude towards Freud. People who saw Freud regularly in those days have tried to convince me that Freud was bitterly against my book from the beginning. This, I repeat, was not to be deduced from his letter or from his subsequent behaviour towards me. I rather think that his pupils and friends were much more antagonistic towards my book than he was himself in the beginning and that it was they who turned him against it, particularly when his opponents took my remarks out of context and quoted me as though I were one of their kind, an enemy of psychoanalysis.

The next thing I did was to attempt to reconcile Freud with Stekel, a foolish attempt because it was doomed from the start to fail.[8] In one of Freud's publications he says of Stekel that his break with him was caused by 'matters which it is hardly possible to make public'. Even more spiteful is the passage in which Freud refers to 'Stekel, so serviceable in the beginning, and afterwards so utterly untrustworthy'.[9] When I learned that this publication was just about to be reprinted for a new edition, I asked Freud to change these hurtful allegations. Freud replied:

> I should like to do you a favour. Of course I could not suppress my criticism of Stekel; even less could I speak about him in a way adequate to his own self-appreciation. However, if the substitution of a milder term for a harsh word can diminish his offence and make himself adopt more polite forms, I do not wish to stand in the way.
>
> Therefore, the very day your letter came I asked about the new printing of my essay, 'History of the Psychoanalytic Movement', and learned that it was too late to do anything. The printing was done and the sheets at the book binder's. So everything has to remain as it is.
>
> Very truly yours,
>
> Freud

Readers who know Freud and his feelings towards Stekel will recognize the diabolic humour of this letter.[10]

In the year 1925 my relations with Stekel came to an end. No sooner did Freud learn about this event, which he had anticipated, than he invited me to come to see him.[11] The immediate motive for this invitation was scientific, as always with Freud. I had sent him a manuscript and he wished to discuss it with me – as in the old days. In this way I came back to the man whose teachings, in my younger years, had struck me with such force, whom I had had to leave and on whom, in defiance and bitterness, I had not called for more than twelve years. When I left him his hair and beard were dark and only slightly grizzled. There he sat, the same man and yet another one. His name had become an idea, and legend was woven about his now snow-white head. I certainly could not argue with him any more. His big cause was mine, my small cause belonged to the past. He said: 'You have not altered much.' I could not say the same about him and kept quiet. I remembered a comparatively young man whom, in 1906, I had once asked to a consultation and who had returned downtown with me afterwards in a one-horse cab. He held a small indiarubber stethoscope in his hand and asked me whether I had been satisfied with him. Incredible that this man's name was Dr Sigmund Freud.

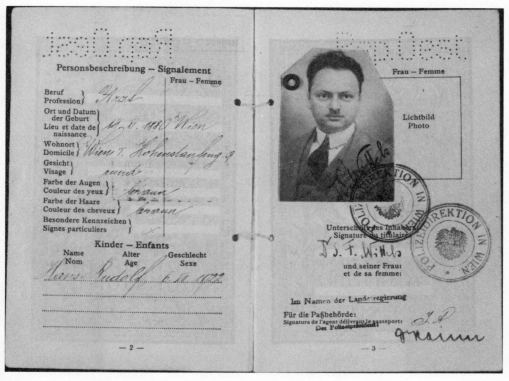

36. Passport with a photograph of Wittels in the early 1920s.

His first question was: 'In order to make things easier for me, tell me in what relation you are to Stekel?' It was always Stekel and clean-cut separation from him that mattered first. When I replied that I did not see him any more, he said: 'I do not ask you why you separated. All I ask is how could you stand him for so long?' There was something vindictive in his voice. I later learned that he blamed Stekel rather than myself for the part of my book which he disliked. I replied: 'You, Professor, could stand him much longer than I.' With this remark I alluded to the twelve to fourteen years during which Stekel had been one of his most prominent pupils, editor of his magazine, spokesman before the public and scientific collaborator. I do not wish to repeat what more he said about Stekel on the occasion of this first conversation with me after the long interval, because it was too bitter. I mention here but one sharp epigram: 'I have committed two crimes in my life: I called attention to cocaine and I introduced Stekel to psychoanalysis.'[12]

Cocaine, though abused by drug addicts, is a drug of paramount importance. Stekel, too, has cured patients, made discoveries, but had, in Freud's eyes, come to be a nuisance. The comparison is, in a way, almost complimentary to Stekel, the assets of cocaine by far outbalancing its dangers.

He asked me why I had not come to him directly instead of having come through Stekel. I said: 'Because you did not invite me.'

He: 'You never asked for an invitation.'

I: 'I wrote to you often.'

He: 'Yes, but your letters were always quarrelsome. Your book was scarcely the right way to bring you back to me, either.'

We then turned to scientific subjects, and I do not remember how long I stayed with him but it was a long time, and he dismissed me with the words: 'I'll be glad if I have won you back for psychoanalysis of the non–Stekel brand.'

We shook hands in grand style and nothing indicated that he resented my book except perhaps, as occurred to me much later, the fact that he did not look in my face when we separated that night.

After this conversation our relations became almost cordial as far as this was possible with one of Freud's 'Nordic' temperament. Between 1925 and 1928 I published four books on psychoanalysis, *Die Technik der Psychoanalyse* (1926), *Die Psychoanalyse: Neue Wege der Seelenkunde* (1927), *Die Befreiung des Kindes* (1927; translated as *Set the Children Free*, London, 1933), and *Die Welt ohne Zuchthaus* (1928). Freud wrote to me: 'Dear Doctor, You probably know that I am biased and like well most of what you write . . .' Or: 'Your little book for which I am very grateful is again very good and contains most excellent passages . . .'

I saw him often in these years. We discussed scientific questions and problems of organization. He sent me patients for treatment and once, in 1927, he even did me the honour of sending me to Munich, when he was invited to lecture on psychoanalysis at the psychiatric institute there and did not feel well enough to accept himself. In the Viennese group of the psychoanalytic association which I frequented, following his wish and my own, I found less benevolence in the beginning. Younger members, particularly, were not sure whether they liked my return. I complained to Freud, who advised me to hold on and show the members that I was a 'valuable acquisition'.

'Some,' he said, 'cannot forgive you your book on me.'

I formally re-entered Freud's organization in 1927.[13] It was no

37. Wittels on holiday with his second wife Lilly, around 1927.

38. Wittels playfully admonishing his schoolboy son, Hans Rudolf (John R. Wittels).

longer what I had abandoned under dramatic circumstances, but had become part of a worldwide international organization. Dr Paul Federn, the vice-chairman, asked me what I intended to do in the matter of my book. I did not consider it urgent because I was under the impression that Freud himself did not take it very seriously. It seemed that way to me then. I promised that I would do something when an occasion presented itself, either in a possible second edition or in another publication in which I could revert to the subject. It was four years since my book's publication and it was no longer in the foreground of public interest.

Freud continued to write me most amiable letters, of which I take the liberty of publishing two more because they are of general interest.[14] His paper on fetishism to which the letters refer was published in 1927, so that the discretion he asked of me is no longer needed.

Semmering (Villa Schueler)
31 July 1927

Dear Doctor,

Perhaps you will be surprised that I ask you for a literary favour. Undoubtedly, however, you will soon understand. In these years I have had the opportunity of carrying out several analyses of fetishism and in each case I found a surprisingly simple solution. I wish to make it the subject of a small communication. But there is somebody who has written a fat volume about the subject. Following the rules of scientific usage, I should read the book and make sure that the shrewd somebody has not found my solution, little likely though this may be. However, I cannot bring myself to do so; I cannot overcome an inner resistance like an instinct for cleanliness. I know well enough that this should not be so, but with age one easily acquires whims and becomes inclined to stick to one's stubbornness.

This time I find useful what I regret so much in your past. You certainly know Stekel's book on fetishism. Is it possible for you to tell me in a few sentences to what conclusions this author comes with regard to the nature and the aim of the fetish? My request is, of course, valid only in case he does express any such conclusion and if it is not too strenuous for you to extract it. In the negative case, notify me on a postal card; in any event be good enough to keep quiet about this confession of an idiosyncrasy which was hard enough for me to acquire.

With cordial greetings,
Yours,

Freud

I am not quite sure whether I succeed in conveying through this translation the sometimes dancing, sometimes grim humour that lies between the lines. At any rate, I was able to tell him that Stekel traced the fetish back to ten different determinants in the unconscious of the pervert. At which came the following letter nine days later:

Dear Doctor,

Many thanks. You have rendered me a good service which makes my publication possible. I will gladly reveal to you in compensation – but keep it still for yourself – that the fetish is not anything tenfold but something very simple, namely, the equivalent for the once imagined and so highly valued penis of the woman (mother's) and therefore a product of defiance against castration and defence against homosexuality.

With cordial greetings,

Yours,

Freud

This is not the place to discuss the value and importance of Freud's statement on fetishism.[15] I would not even reproduce these letters here, were it not for the documentation of Freud's cordial attitude. And even that might sound boastful and I would not speak about it, were it not important to contrast this attitude with events which will be reported in the following chapter.

9

America: Making Amends

In 1928 I was invited to lecture and to teach psychoanalysis in America.[1] I asked Freud what he thought of this idea, and the following was his answer:

20 April 1928

Dear Doctor,
   My advice is unequivocal.[2] If you have connections in the USA, the prospect of earning money there by teaching and analysing, do not miss the opportunity. You know the disconsolate economic conditions in Vienna and also how unlikely a change is in this respect in the near future. Constant worry about earning a living is not so good for the character either.
   Your additional purpose of fighting Adler there is of course very praiseworthy. Do not make it a main issue, because this shallow short–cut of analysis is bound to please Americans by its positive content as well as by what it denies. However, America is so vast that there is room for all antagonistic doctrines side by side . . .

Wishing you much success,

Yours,

Freud

I accepted the invitation from America and made myself ready for the crossing. When I was able to tell Freud that my projected visit to America had become a matter of certainty, he wrote:

11 July 1928

Dear Doctor,
   I feel tremendously reassured by learning authentically that

February 25, 1930

My dear Dr. Wittels:

I am instructed by the Board of Directors of
the New School for Social Research to inform you that your
appointment as Lecturer in Psychoanalysis and Psychotherapy
has been extended through the year 1930-1931.

We are much gratified that you will be with
us again next year, and we are sure that your work will be
even more successful than it has been in the last two years.

Please send me a line, at your convenience,
signifying your acceptance.

Yours truly,

Director

Dr. Fritz Wittels
1045 Park Avenue
New York, N. Y.

39. Letter from Alvin Johnson, Director
of the New School for Social Research,
25 February 1930.

you will escape Viennese pauperism by your trip to New
York. The smaller my personal influence has grown to
improve the position of my younger friends, the more do I feel
afflicted by it. I deeply appreciate your intention of paving the
way for similar appointments for other members of our
society. Let us hope that you will be successful in that. I
believe that I know the situation over there very well from
reports and will gladly tell you what I consider expedient. Do
not be surprised if my advice sounds different from before.

I am very much pleased to hear that you share my opinion
of the relative value of analysis for medical therapy, pedagogy
and general cultural education without restriction. However,
should you present yourself over there with a programme in
favour of lay-analysis, you will incur the embittered enmity of
the medical analysts and increase their distrust towards later
visitors from our circle. This point cannot be carried through
in America. On the other hand, it is very worthwhile to work
against Adlerianism which has spread quickly because of his
repeatedly successful performances; in this you can be sure of
support from our group there which has proved absolutely
dependable on this point. Of course I do not mean to say that

you should disavow or keep secret your position in the layman's question; but make no platform of it. These primitives have little interest in science not directly convertible into practice. The worst of the American way is their so-called broadmindedness through which they even feel themselves to be magnanimous and superior to us narrowminded Europeans; this is actually, of course, but a convenient veiling of their complete lack of judgement. They concoct – almost in the way of unconscious tendencies – a compromise or a mixture of analysis, Jungian mysticism and Adlerianism, a shameful nonsense, naturally, and well deserving of your derision. This accomplishment is made easier for them by the fact that they have read as much as nothing of the original publications, having neither the time nor desire to do so.

But you will see for yourself and act accordingly.

My best wishes for the outer and inner success of your enterprise travel with you.

Cordially, yours

Freud

I answered this letter – he was absent from Vienna as always in summer – and I received one more letter from him before I left Europe:[3]

7 August 1928

Dear Doctor,

Sure, the American and psychoanalysis are often so ill-adapted for one another that one is reminded of Grabbe's parable, 'as though a raven were to put on a white shirt'. It is not yet clear why this is so. Perhaps you will find out. One thing is certain: you will not change the American. It is best to remain reservedly on the pedestal of one's scientific nature and let people and events pass by.

With best wishes for your trip,

Yours,

Freud

I left the shores of France in September 1928, and no sooner had I touched American soil than I felt enveloped by the intoxicating hospitality, curiosity, the tremendous *élan vital* of a country in 'prosperity'. It seems to me that a description of my experiences in America belongs elsewhere; I am not engaged here in writing a full autobiography, but only in that little part of it which concerns my relation to a great man who came to be of paramount importance in my life. Just one word: America in an incredibly short time became my home.[4] I was and am happy here and I did not share in the least Freud's strangely hostile opinion of the Americans. After a month or two I sent him a report which he acknowledged in this letter:[5]

11 November 1928

Dear Doctor,

I received your peculiarly reserved letter and read it with satisfaction. It is full of meaning and free from illusions. I feel particularly reassured to hear that you are sure of the material aim of your American trip; perhaps you did not quite believe in the seriousness of my interest. Your judgements about persons and conditions seem to me to be correct throughout. Over there they are not analysts in our sense but psychiatrists also using analysis in their work. No cultural perspectives exist for them; we cannot help that. A certain mixture of ignorance and irreverence is characteristic of American publications. We cannot hope for scientific contributions from there, nor for money for our aims, so useful to all.

If you want me to say a few introductory words for you, the only way is to let me know what you wish to have, to prescribe it to me, so to speak.

I was somewhat surprised to hear what you say about the fading away of Adlerianism. I should have thought that so shallow a simplification of difficult problems would particularly recommend itself to the American spirit, somewhat like Behaviourism. We can hardly overlook the fact that the American in science, too, is dominated by his political passions; therefore the Monroe Doctrine and the belief that old man Europe has no right to speak out but must be curbed. This was probably the main psychological motive for America's interference in the war.

I have been in Berlin in the meanwhile, where Professor Schroeder has made a plate for me which makes life more bearable, without, though, providing ease.

Expecting more news from you and with best wishes for your success.

Yours,

Freud

It seems to me that, after all the years of undisturbed friendship and the assurance of these letters, I had a right to assume that Freud had finally become a reliable fatherly figure in my life, one to whom I could talk and with whom I could discuss not personal affairs, but all that pertained to psychoanalysis and his person, so inseparable from the science he created. In those days American publishers were after me, and one of them suggested that I rearrange my biography for a second edition. I looked through my book and came to the conclusion that I had better write a totally new book. It seemed to me impossible to change the old one without entirely devitalizing it. Its ambivalent spirit was not eradicable. I did what seemed to me the natural thing to do: I described my dilemma in my next report to Freud. His immediate answer to my letter follows:

8 January 1929

Dear Doctor,
    I am writing you immediately after receiving your letter of December 28th in which a passage is inexplicable to me and makes me apprehensive.
    This is your text: 'They are asking here for a second edition of my sin of 1923 (the biography) and you can imagine my embarrassment. I think and think and cannot find the right way. Perhaps I had better let the book go out of print.'
    Well, I do not understand your embarrassment and think that the right way cannot be missed. All the antecedents point to it. Let me present a short summary: In 1923, without asking me for authorization, you published a biography of me which, in many respects, drew a hateful caricature of my person. It had great success in the public because of your gift of good presentation, because of the interest in your object and because it was a sop to the world's gossipy tendencies. It is true that you were then in no personal relation to me and were under no obligation. I was sorry that you had written this book. I had thought that a certain esteem of me had remained with you from previous contacts. I was not conscious of having done you an injustice. I had no idea that, under the influence of Stekel, you had succeeded in building up such a picture of injustice. For this aim you had to forget the real cause of our breach. It is odd enough that you were able to do that. Let me be cautious and remind you of it. During your brawl with K. Kraus you had simultaneously written lampoons against and

friendly letters to him. When asked about this, you answered defiantly that you had felt ambivalent and would not allow yourself to be deprived of the privilege of acting according to your feelings. To us, however, not only to myself, this refusal of a cultural correction of an impulsive attitude seemed to be incompatible with the duties of the analyst to the public . . . [there follows a passage on and against Stekel.]

I took the damage inflicted upon me by your biography with the indifference acquired in the course of my life. Somehow I did not even grow angry at you because revenge is no necessity of mine, and because I was still pleased with you from before. I wrote to you and myself corrected a few errors in your biography. Shortly afterwards, you could not stand Stekel any longer and made steps aiming at an admission to the group. I tried to pave the way for you and not I, but the members of the group, remonstrated with you about the sin of your biography. You declared – so I was told – that you had changed your mind and promised to express this in a possible second edition.

Now the occasion for this second edition has occurred. One should expect that you would be glad to fulfil your promise and to tell the public about your better understanding. Instead you say that you feel embarrassed and cannot see the right way. I can, you write, easily imagine that. No, I cannot. Doubts and difficulties, if any, have not emerged anew; you must have known them when you gave your promise . . . [there follows again a passage on Stekel.]

I considered it my duty to present these considerations for your decision.

Freud

I felt sick when I read this letter. Contrary to my impression, Freud, it seemed, had forgotten and forgiven nothing. My readers know from the previous chapters of this book what Freud meant when he wrote about my lampoon and the friendly letters to Kraus. I have given the reader a conscientious and full account of my 'ambivalence'. There was, as I saw it, a misunderstanding which I could never and which to this day I cannot correct. It is true that I was very fond of Kraus for a time, but we separated, he insulted me and I decided to take my revenge – while I was at work upon it I felt that I wanted a reconciliation and I wrote him several notes to this effect. When he did not answer, I felt that I owed it to myself to go ahead with my revenge action, i.e., my novel. I published it two years after my so-called 'love letters' when there was no longer any possibility of contact with him. This was the extent of my ambivalence. While I can see clearly that I should not have published my novel, I never blamed myself for the 'ambivalence' of the situation. I am exposing the entire matter at such length because of the weak spot in my case: I forgot the letters. This phenomenon of forgetting followed the mechanism made famous by Nietzsche: 'This is what you have done, says your memory. I cannot possibly have done it, says your pride. And by and by the memory gives in.'[6] It is not pleasant to remember that one has failed to find favour with a man who has hurt one and whom one should therefore avoid – to say the least.

The main object of Freud's letter was quite incomprehensible to me. I was definitely about to do something in the matter of the biography. For what other reason could I have written to Freud about it? He, a literary man himself, was to understand the difficulty of changing the book without complete dis-integration. At that time my relation and my gratitude to him were such that I would have gone through fire and water for him and I thought he knew that. All America reverberated with my enthusiasm for him and his work. It seemed to me that this was the best way to show the world my change of view and to atone for my previous action which, after all, did not by any means contradict my work for Freud in America. With sincerity and every conviction I had proclaimed to crowded halls in America's many cities the greatness of the man Freud and how admirable his work was. I cabled a long message to Vienna asking for further explanation but no answer came from angry Jupiter.

For a long time I was at a loss to understand what could have brought about this metamorphosis of my teacher and fatherly friend. I thought myself a man ready to recognize my mistakes unless I was blinded by passions, but here I felt myself blameless. I later learned from Freud that people had written him that they did not appreciate my work in New York. But that was not it. Among the letters that came to him, however, was one from a colleague who wrote that I had spoken at a private dinner in her house about an impending second edition of the biography and had said: 'What shall I do? I am afraid of Stekel.' I have a letter from Freud in which he admits that it was this remark I was reported to have made that angered him. But there was no mention of this in his irate letter.

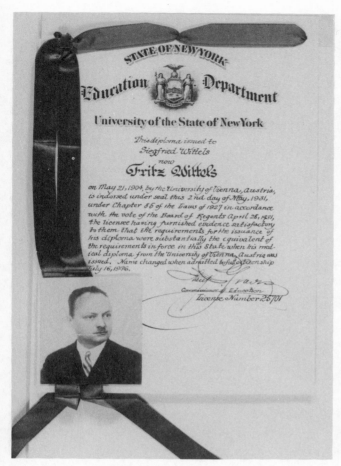

STATE OF NEW YORK

Education Department

University of the State of New York

This diploma issued to
Siegfried Wittels
now
Fritz Wittels

on May 21, 1904, by the University of Vienna, Austria,
is endorsed under seal this 2nd day of May, 1931,
under Chapter 85 of the Laws of 1927 in accordance
with the vote of the Board of Regents April 26, 1931,
the licensee having furnished evidence satisfactory
to them that the requirements for the issuance of
his diploma were substantially the equivalent of
the requirements in force in this State when his med-
ical diploma from the University of Vienna, Austria was
issued. Name changed when admitted to full citizenship
July 16, 1936.

Commissioner of Education
License Number 25701

40. Licence from the State of
New York recognizing
Wittels's Viennese medical
qualifications, 2 May 1931.

Here is an explanation – or an attempt at an explanation. In 1910 I published *Ezekiel*. My two fathers, Freud and Kraus, knew about it in advance and tried to prevent the publication. Kraus had turned enemy before, Freud became hostile when he saw that he could not succeed in supressing my book. In 1923 I published another book, the biography, of which Freud knew nothing in advance, while the place of Kraus was this time occupied by Stekel, whom Freud despised even more than he disliked Kraus and his influence on me. When Freud saw what I had done, he did not repeat his behaviour of 1910. On the contrary, he made my ambivalent book the starting point of my *rapprochement* to psychoanalysis and in this way made possible my separation from Stekel, the new Kraus figure. He buried his anger. But it burst out five years later when, because I still seemed to be in touch with Stekel, he came to the conclusion

41. Wittels
the successful
physician, around
1930.

that I was not to be trusted.

My repetition can be explained in two equations. The one is
my own Father = Kraus = *Ezekiel* and the other is Father =
Freud = Biography. These equations interfere with each other
and are responsible for the ambivalence of the biography. I had
to separate from Kraus in order to find my way to Freud and did
not. I had to separate for the same reason from Stekel and, in
doing so, found my way to Freud. I did not know, and perhaps I
could not know after years of Freud's cordial behaviour, that I

42. Sketch of Wittels by an unidentified Viennese artist, 1930.

had planted a time bomb which had to explode at a predestined moment. It did explode when the fuse called Stekel was touched. It is amusing to note the repetition of still another motif in the drama: a woman who served as intermediary was again a character in the final act. She explained the somewhat gossipy letter, incidentally, by saying that she felt she had to warn Freud of a possible disappointment.

It was not easy for Freud to forgive and come back to people with whom he had severed relations. His friends told me that I was the only exception and that he had broken one of his fundamental principles in my case. I doubt whether I was the only one, but there were certainly not many. Why, then, this sudden change? I had a talk with him about this question four years afterwards in 1933, which I will report later. There was not the slightest reason why I should have been afraid of Stekel, who lived four thousand miles away and whom I had not seen since 1925. True, in my biography, I gave Stekel a better standing than did the Freudians and later insight considerably altered my views. Under these circumstances I felt it was better to let the world forget some of the things that I had said in my book on Freud, including a somewhat distorted appreciation of Stekel. This was one of the reasons why I wished to write a new book on Freud. I did so two years later: *Freud and His Time* (New York, 1931).

At the end of April 1929, I was back in Vienna and found Freud far from reconciled. An exchange of letters followed. One of them ends with the characteristic words: 'I quite agree with your resolution to let the book go out of print without renovation. The matter is unpleasant to me throughout because it deals again with my famous "thirst for revenge". If you like, we will not mention it any more. I am looking forward to your presence at our next evening in my house, May third. Yours, Freud.'

This looked like the end of the affair, but it wasn't. Freud was cool to me from that time on, and I felt that I had to do something drastic in the matter. I could not well bear the idea that I had filled our great father in Vienna with bitterness. There was but one consideration which made me wait. People would say about me: 'He wants success, has become "orthodox" and hence he revokes.' I waited four more years, therefore, until there was no longer any doubt that I was well established in America and completedly independent of any organization, Freudian or otherwise, and then, in 1933, I published a detailed revision of my biography in three distinguished scientific magazines, two in America and one in Vienna. This revision left nothing to be desired in terms of confession and revocation.

Here is the beginning of my revision of 1933:[7]

In 1923 I published a biography of Sigmund Freud which appeared in English translation in 1924, and which, because of the nature of the book, received wide attention in scientific circles. It is to the present day cited by psychologists in their lectures and publications, and I have reason to fear that a number of psychologists, rather remote from the field of psychoanalysis, derive a major part of their knowledge of this subject from my book. This has been a source of embarrassment to me for I have, in the ten years that have elapsed since the appearance of the book, changed my opinion considerably concerning psychoanalysis and its founder, and therefore can no longer stand sponsor for the errors and misrepresentations which I have come to recognize as such.

It occurred to me that I might make reparation by publishing a new edition of the biography. As I went over the book, however, for this purpose, I realized that it would be a sheer impossibility for me so to transform the work that it would express adequately my present position in regard to Freud and his school to which I belong. The tone of the book throughout is a striking example of ambivalence and it is beyond my power to entirely eradicate it. Passages in which I pay high tribute to Freud alternate with others which hurt not only his work, a brunt which every scholar must bear, but his personality. The book is so written that it is perforce welcome to all who seek rationalization for their own ambivalent attitude towards psychoanalysis.

I have since given expression in various books and articles to my change of view, yet none of these works has been able to obliterate the impression that was created upon scientific circles by my publication of 1923. I had hoped – and with some ground for the hope – that the publication would gradually fall into oblivion. For this reason I kept silent, thinking it best to return no more to this youthful indiscretion. While, however, the purely scientific portion of my book, with its truth and errors, scarcely needs further comment, it is precisely the personal content of the book which to my chagrin continually reappears.

In my book I remark that Freud has an overwhelmingly high opinion of himself – the Jehovah complex; that he is a despot who will not tolerate deviations from his system; that he brings disciples into hypnotic dependence upon him; that he repels his friends and especially if they are men of importance themselves; that he rarely abandons errors which are obviously such, is, the book continues, not free from cryptomnesia, and his psychoanalytic policy pursues ways not always above reproach. These words of disapproval – condensed here to a few lines – are spread throughout my book, over 287 pages, and are again and again interspersed with frank hero worship. However, this does not serve to mitigate them; quite to the contrary. The reader inevitably arrives at the conclusion: Behold one who so honours him, and yet . . .

The letter which Freud wrote me after the German edition had appeared, and with which in an authorized abstract I prefaced the English translation, shows that the Professor, astonishingly unmoved, scarcely noticed the defamatory passages and approached this biography, of which before its appearance he knew nothing, with complete objectivity, as though it had nothing to do with his person but only with a matter which was, in general, science, in particular, psychoanalysis. Yet he did more than that. I had been pursuing my way apart from his pupils for a number of years – five years of war had lengthened the time. After the appearance of my book, which certainly was anything but a good introduction, he drew me back to his school and gave me the opportunity to relearn and to see for myself whether my opinion of his personality and his teaching was correct or not. I may say that never have I met a worker who so completely and effortlessly entered into his work . . .

Many letters came from Freud's adherents and sympathizers congratulating me on this 'frank and courageous' step. Others expressed their bewilderment, feeling, apparently, that one could not depend on my opinion, and openly wondered if I were not ashamed of myself over this *Pater Peccavi*. I must admit that I was not at all ashamed; on the contrary, rarely did a scientific paper give me more pleasure than this revision. My superego looked over my shoulder and kept on nodding while I wrote.

This piece of work was again like a private letter to Freud. The following summer, 1933, I saw him in Vienna. He looked old and weak, but his mind was young and he was still ready for battle. I asked him whether my revision had contented him at last. To my intense surprise he answered, 'No.' He admitted that I had gone far in my revocations, perhaps, even, too far, because he did not deserve all this praise. Why, then, was he not satisfied with it? He replied with an anecdote. The older he grew, the more he became inclined to express his opinions in the form of the parable; it was an Oriental habit of which he had reached mastery.

'Ivan, the Terrible,' he said, 'one day exterminated his entire

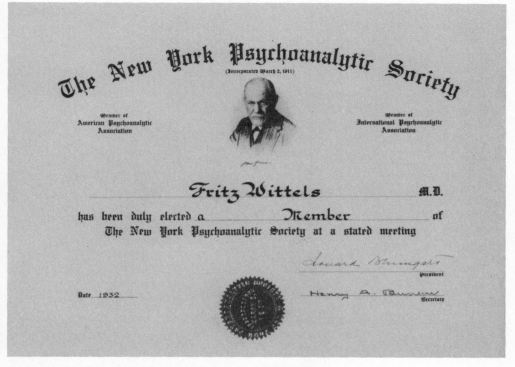

The New York Psychoanalytic Society
(Incorporated March 2, 1911)

Member of
American Psychoanalytic
Association

Member of
International Psychoanalytic
Association

Fritz Wittels   M.D.

has been duly elected a   Member   of
The New York Psychoanalytic Society at a stated meeting

President

Date 1932

Secretary

43.   Membership certificate of the New York Psychoanalytic Society, 1932.

family. A short time later he prostrated himself on a lawn, received the blessings of the clerics and, because he had thus atoned for his sin, was declared a saint. So you. First you publish a book which makes you famous, then you revoke and the world murmurs: "Look at him; what a man he is, what bold frankness he shows!" In this way you enjoy your pleasure twice.'

A serious consideration lay behind the joke. I asked: 'In your opinion, what should I have done?' He replied: 'You should have published a second edition, a dull book, of which little notice would have been taken, and there would have been no pleasure for you in that.'

In this half-jocose attitude he meant to express the futility of the whole episode. I, however, was serious. I repeated that a second edition was not possible and explained why I felt as I did. He replied with another anecdote. 'There once was a tailor who promised a patron a suit which would not wrinkle with the movements of the body. The patron ordered the suit but when it was ready for wear he found that it wrinkled just like any ordinary suit. He refused, therefore, to pay for the suit and

4. Wittels towards the end of his career.

patron and tailor went together to the *cadi*. There the tailor presented his defence: "Your Honour, everybody knows that it is impossible to make a suit with these qualities." "That may be so," answered the *cadi*, "but I convict you just the same. You should not have promised it."'

In this same talk he mentioned that others had written about him and some of them with undisguised hostility. I had set a bad example, he said. When I asked him if he felt that, had it not been for me, these others would not have written as they did, he said: 'Anyone who deflowers a girl says that – if not I, someone else would have done it.'

He was in a good mood. I asked him why he had not told me at the start how much he disliked my book and how hurt he felt by it. He gave the following tripartite explanation of his friendly reaction in this conversation of 1933: 'First,' he said, 'I was sick at the time and felt that I did not have much to do any more with the squabbles of this world. Second, you had written this book under the influence of Stekel in order to annoy me, so it was not proper to show that I was annoyed. Lastly, I knew you to be a gifted man, I saw that you wanted to return to psychoanalysis and I considered it my duty to help you . . .'

He changed the subject suddenly and growing angry, said: 'It wasn't the biography alone; there are those letters that you wrote to Kraus – regular "love letters", while you were occupied in attacking him. This was very unfair of you, and not only that, it was an act of cowardice.'

I hardly trusted my ears. 'Professor,' I said, 'do you realize that this was twenty-five years ago?' He made a soothing gesture towards me. 'I know,' he said, 'but you were close to me . . .'

He was tired and I left him. It was my last meeting with him. I lived in America at that time and I felt that I had no further business in Vienna, which was slowly preparing herself to receive the Führer and to expel one of her greatest citizens . . .

10

Freud in America

Freud died in London on 23 September 1939. The history of his last years is an epic of its own, and I hope it will be written up by someone closer to him than I could have been.

We were told in school, long years ago, that when the Roman soldiers broke into the home of Archimedes, the ancient mathematician stood above the geometrical figures he had drawn in the sand and warned the soldiers: 'Do not disturb my circles!', and went on figuring. Freud's reply to his expulsion from Vienna, his home for more than eighty years, was a book, his last, *Moses and Monotheism*. He proved himself scientist and philosopher to the very end. When his Viennese lawyer came to visit him in London, Freud said to him: 'I presume you are now going back to that city of yours – what was its name? . . .'

After 1934 I had no further personal contact with Freud. The few more letters we exchanged add nothing to my story, which has come to its end. But before I do close my narrative here, there are some brief words to be added with regard to my position in America after the master's death. I remarked in my introduction to this book that for a while I contemplated calling it 'A Story of Ambivalence'. At other times I thought it might well be called 'The Story of an "Orthodox" Freudian', since that is what some people in America call me now.[1] It seems a strange end for a rebellious spirit like mine. Who could have foretold that from a history of those early years? I cannot deny, none-theless, that I am bitterly opposed to the attempts of a few former followers of Freud to wreck the great man's work under the pretence of continuing and developing it. Calling upon political passions and terms, they name me as a reactionary and themselves liberal reformers. They call on all 'broadminded' Americans to support their truly scientific and progressive spirit and they denounce me as a rigid believer in a creed instead of a

45. Freud in exile in London in 1938.

debatable doctrine. I, on the other hand, see clearly that they are trying to set back the hands of the clock to the time before Freud. The revolutionary spirit – if this political term must be used – is still on the side of Freud, and what these others attempt to establish is a Bourbon restoration. For this reason I stay put and for the time being I am enjoying my characterization as 'orthodox' – certainly the last thing on earth I ever expected to be called.

It is by no means uncommon in the history of mankind for ambitious lesser figures to consider, when a great teacher dies, that their day has come. Such was the case with Buddha, whose teachings disappeared from his homeland, India, after his death, and with Confucius, who for years was forgotten in China. There is, of course, a fundamental difference between a religious faith and a scientific doctrine, but both Buddha and Confucius were much less religious prophets than revolutionizing philosophers whose teachings were deliberately destroyed by their erstwhile disciples, ambitious younger men who perceived that their former masters' teachings were unpalatable to the boards of regents on whom promotion and career depended. These doctrines were for some time entirely eclipsed, but they reappeared to shine for ever like a mountain from behind a passing cloud. Goethe said: 'It is of no use to cross the ocean of ignorance with the ship of truth; behind her the waves close in and everything is again as it was before.'[2] I cannot hold with this pessimistic sigh, but I must admit that there are times when it would appear to be true – temporarily.

Freud's work does not need me and my small contribution to be safe in America. The great majority of the younger generation of psychoanalysts in this country seem to understand that Freud's magnificent discoveries have enriched the world with a quality which will not be lost. There are only a few former psychoanalysts who try to concoct compromises by discarding the fundamentals of Freud's creation. They hope thereby to earn the praise of the professors of academic psychology, of the social workers downtown and of the main body of American physicians, to whom Freud's statements have remained unacceptable. These attempts are doomed to failure because Freud's edifice is of such a kind that even the smallest building block therein makes the non–Freudians feel ill at ease. The majority of American physicians feel about Freud the way a notorious police president in the Kaiser's Prussia felt about the liberals when he said: 'Your course does not suit us and that is all.' Our compromisers betray Freudian fundamentals and, losing in this way the solid psychoanalytic support of our own side, they are building a bridge into the nowhere. Nobody really wants them; they fulfil no need.

There is, for example, Freud's 'pansexualism'. A few of my colleagues have sacrificed Freud's main discovery, for which he was made to suffer ignobly and around which the ceaseless struggle of forty years still continued at his death. His discoveries in this field were published in his manifesto, *Three Essays on the Theory of Sexuality*, in 1905. They are well known all over the world, have revolutionized and have fired expression in literature and art, and have enriched the thinking and the work of teachers, philosophers and even that of the clergy. Must we repeat his statements that all men are bisexual, that children have a sex life of their own culminating in the Oedipus complex, that sexual activity is by no means confined exclusively to the genitalia? A new method was found to help nervous people, and countless practising psychoanalysts have accepted as an essential of their work these theories of Freud's, the truth of which they daily see demonstrated before their eyes. Before Freud, only the act for the purpose of propagation was called a sex act. Freud

46. Wittels in 1949, photographed by his son.

saw in our sexuality the god Eros, the constructive principle, in
manifold forms. Beauty, fragrance, music, the mouth, the teeth,
eyes, skin, muscles, all the mucous membranes have to play
their role in this magnificent symphony – and the nervous man
is nervous because of a crippling process somewhere in this
polyphonous concert.

A few formerly prominent psychoanalysts – not 'ambivalent'
men like me, but pupils whom Freud especially trusted –
suddenly and to our amazement began to deny Freud's

discoveries in the field of sex.[3] After many years of teaching
what they, like myself, had considered to be their mission in
science, they joined the medical practitioners of Arkansas in
saying: it does not make sense to call anything sexual but the
propagative act of two adult humans of different sex. The lips?
Why, they obviously belong to the digestive tract. Bisexuality?
Why, obviously a man is a man and a woman a woman except
for a few freaks of nature. Oedipus complex? Who has ever
heard of a boy who really wanted to make love to his mother,
and if he did feel that way, what right have we to call this
sexual? A silly chorus of Freud-killers, incorporated, quack an
ugly concert for the sake of reducing Freud's tremendous work
in the field of sex to the status of such knowledge at the time
before this great man began his investigations.

Perhaps there is no real danger for Freud's work, and then
again perhaps there is. The soil in which psychoanalysis grew
and expanded has been destroyed – for a century. Its future
depends entirely on America, which means that either there will
be no psychoanalysis in the future, or it will have to thrive in
America, which is a country that is still virginal soil in
psychological matters. May the expression of a few misgivings
regarding this future therefore be permitted.

America's magnificent scientific spirit is as yet devoted to
dimensions, to measuring and weighing, to figures and statistics;
in a word, to quantities. Quality is less well comprehended. It
may be that this young civilization is not sufficiently seasoned to
develop the concept of quality which dominates values in art,
religion, and, as we know now, in science, too. One of these
qualities is scientific tact, reverence for the genius and his work.
Another quality is beauty. I spoke with a boy of eight who had
come here from Switzerland a short time ago. He was still full of
his Swiss patriotism: the highest mountains, the vast lake of
Geneva, the big bridge in Lausanne – all quantitative values. Our
great lakes of the Middle West were pointed out to him on a
map, and he asked somewhat suspiciously: 'Is Lake Michigan
bigger than Lake Geneva?' When the answer was: 'Sure, much
bigger', a shadow came over his face, for his patriotic sense was
hurt. I tried to comfort him by emphasizing that the Swiss lake
was much more beautiful, bordered as it was with vineyards,
upland pastures, and snow-encrusted peaks, but I did not
succeed. Beauty is a quality which cannot be measured, and such
a quality meant very little to this youngster to whom dimensions
meant everything.

Europeans are probably biased against America when they believe that grown-up Americans, too, are fascinated by figures and less by the essence, the intrinsic nature of unmeasurable qualities. They can understand the highest buildings as such, the longest aqueducts, the deepest chasms, the mightiest dams, the largest cities with enormous cinemas and opera houses. They wish to have the costliest paintings in the biggest museums or in the mansions of the richest men. They are less qualified for a scientific approach to the irrational world of the soul, which they either reject as not scientific or accept in the form of pseudoscientific, typically American doctrines such as Christian Science, Buchmanism or, further West, as evangelical doctrine from the lips of white-robed priestesses.[4]

After 1910, J.B. Watson's Behaviourism became America's representative psychology.[5] The merits and intellectual honesty of Watson and his collaborators cannot be denied. They said: the *stimulus* goes in and the *response* comes out. These two can be measured. What is in between? Thoughts, desires, fears and other qualities in which the Behaviourists displayed no interest. No scientific approach to these 'imponderables' is possible with their yardsticks as instruments. I admit that they have changed their attitude, although this has most likely come about under Freud's influence. But Watson was once asked in my presence what the human conscious was, and he answered in his forceful way: 'I do not know and I do not care!' Here is where Freud comes in: he cares and he was able to tell us a few things about the ego of man and its dependence on inner powers. Freud made most interesting discoveries with his 'introspective' method. Experimental psychology with its scales and meters in gleaming chrome and crystal laboratories could not hail the same world-shaking success. All they had to say about psychoanalysis was that our way of investigation was not scientific. But let us compare the two methods.

A few years ago I attended a lecture announced as 'Psychology of Success'. Success is a subject in which psychoanalysis, too, is keenly interested. Many people complain about repeated failures, despite hard and honest work, and some of them punish themselves by their failures. Such people we call masochistic. Some people are 'wrecked by success'. In short, here is a topic of great importance, which looms large in the dreams of mankind: all of us yearn to be successful.

On entering the lecture hall, I saw that I had stepped into the realm of Behaviourism. The blackboard was covered with figures and diagrams, and the lecturer stood before it, pointer in hand. Problem posed: if you place a piece of chocolate high enough to make it impossible for a child of four, five, six and so on years to reach it (i.e. to have success), how many minutes and how often will a certain child continue its unsuccessful attempts? If you repeat the experiment the next day or after several days, five, ten, twenty days, how many children will not even try to reach the unattainable – boys, girls, four, five, six and so on years old? But we are not yet through. How many will try again, but not as long as on the first day? Partial or interspersed success can also be studied by letting them have some of the chocolate. *Voilà*! Here was the 'scientific' approach to the psychology of success – a statistician's paradise.

The professors' needles dance on sooted drums, guineapigs and crayfish are hypnotized, and the results are published in fat volumes printed with the financial support of generous sponsors in universities and foundations. Freud's apparatus was characterized by not being apparatus – a couch and a chair, the patient lying on the couch and the analyst listening to what the sick man's heart led him to say about his anxieties, his happiness and unhappiness, his love and his hate. A very different method indeed.

There was a man who once suggested to Freud that he join the ranks of the measuring and therefore scientific psychologists. There was his libido theory, for instance, which conceived the libido to be a limited energy, coveting and creating pleasure. Why not measure it like electricity, which is expressed in volts, amperes and ohms? The unit of the libido could be called *one Freud* in the discoverer's honour. Freud pretended to be alarmed, complimented the man on his idea and ended with the words: 'I do not understand enough of physics to express a reliable judgement in the matter. But if I am permitted to ask a favour, do not call your unit by my name.' With unfailing wit he added that he hoped to die with 'unmeasured libido'.

There is, of course, no reason why we should not measure libido, if we can, the ideal of the statistician being to express a man's nature as 50 per cent normal sexuality, 15 per cent homosexuality, 10 per cent sadism and an equal amount of masochism, with the remaining percentages scattered in different forms of sublimation. Not only is there so far no appropriate method for this purpose, but we feel with Freud that we have better things to do. We are getting close to the essence of human nature in a direct approach. The meaning of Freud's psychoanalysis is a scientific method with which the psychic quality in man can be explored, that very quality which before Freud was only felt in religious contemplation, in art and literature. It seems that physicians and biologists are slow in accepting this quality. They do not believe that it is possible to formulate it, to operate with its parts without referring to the body, to the brain, the nerves, to one of the many glands or to biochemistry. Psychoanalysis does just that without hesitation. Physicians equipped with stethoscope, microscope and all the other scopes look askance at this new and purely psychological tendency. Is it not a romantic return to mysticism, to the Holy Ghost? What is this libido, the instrument of all creative power which Freud himself compared with the ancient Greek god Eros? What is a scientist to do with the concept of instincts studied by psychoanalysis in detail with all their metamorphoses and disguises? It is the inner world which we describe. The external world and our dependence on it was known always. Good or bad luck in life, danger, sharp competition, absence or presence of love, good or bad health, these we always knew, and called our fate. Freud added to this the concept of the inner man who determines his destiny from within to such an extent that the importance of good and ill fortune from without is almost nullified. Hence the old philosophy, perhaps the deepest truth, that we owe real joy only to our own heart. The mission of psychoanalysis is to make our hearts free from anxiety and guilt and free for joy. In this realm there is no room for inches or for ounces.

★

Freud's last work on Moses was written almost in the transparency of transfiguration.[6] According to this book Moses was an Egyptian prince who tried to save the lofty spirit of Echnaton's sun religion, which the Egyptian priests had destroyed after the death of this enlightened Pharaoh. He taught it to the Jews in flaming words and made the new religion the instrument of their liberation from slavery. Unfortunately the religion of a god whom nobody could see, who had not even a name and in addition imposed harsh frustrating laws upon his people, proved too much for the liberated slaves. They killed their leader in the desert and returned to the gods of gold, of brass and of stone. Moses' highly spiritual doctrine was forgotten, and idolatry re-established. A whispered tradition of Moses' Echnaton religion survived, however, and after the passage of centuries prophets appeared who taught the original doctrine in all its glory. There were many prophets, an uninterrupted chain of them never to end any more.

It seems to me as though Freud foresaw that his immediate followers, draped in the tirades of progressive reformers, appeasers and ambitious careerists, would attempt the destruction of his system. But prophets will again appear . . .

Commentary: The Wittels Memoirs in Context

The Commentary is divided into four sections followed by an index:

- A. Acknowledgements
- B. Sources
- C. Publications by Fritz Wittels
- D. Notes on the Text

A. ACKNOWLEDGEMENTS

The Editor would like to express his thanks to the following individuals and institutions for their assistance:

John R. Wittels, for consenting to publication of his father's memoirs and for providing information about the Wittels family; Peter Gay, for guidance about Wittels's literary estate; Sophie Schick, for generously sharing the findings of her own research about Karl Kraus; Murray Hall, Gerald Krieghofer, Silke Hassler and John G. Ramsay, for help in tracing and reconstructing the identity of Irma Karczewska; Gerhard Fichtner, for information about Freud's correspondence; W. E. Yates, for identifying the source of Nestroy quotations; Nicholas Boyle, for identifying a quotation from Goethe; Karen Owen, for skilfully transferring Wittels's text on to word processor; Francis Clark-Lowes, for helpful comments on the edited text; and Candida Brazil for editing.

The Abraham A. Brill Library, for generously allowing access to Wittels's unpublished papers; The Library of Congress in Washington, for information about Freud's correspondence; The Freud Museum in London, for information about Freud's library; Sigmund Freud Copyrights, for permission to publish letters from

Freud, translated by Wittels; The Vienna City Library (Wiener Stadt- und Landesbibliothek), for permitting access to a wide range of research materials, including unpublished letters; the Austrian Theatre Museum (Österreichisches Theatermuseum) in Vienna, for details of productions of Grillparzer's *Die Ahnfrau* at the Burgtheater; and the University of Sussex at Brighton, and Gonville and Caius College, Cambridge, for supporting research visits to Austria and the United States.

B. SOURCES

In 1970 the literary estate of Fritz Wittels was deposited by the executors of his widow, Mrs Poldi Goetz Wittels, in the Abraham A. Brill Library at the New York Psychoanalytic Institute, 247 East Eighty-Second Street, New York, NY 10028. The collection consists of six substantial boxes containing a total of sixty-seven folders, together with two larger-format portfolios. In addition to diaries, correspondence and miscellaneous manuscripts, the collection includes the typescripts of no less than six projected books, all of which have hitherto remained unpublished.

The present edition is a conflation from two different sources. The main source is entitled 'Wrestling with the Man: The Story of a Freudian', a relatively polished but incomplete typescript with the page numbers 6–13(a) and 80–155 and 157–201. The table of contents for this volume, reproduced in Fig 47, indicates that three of the chapters originally envisaged are missing: 'Idealism' (Chapter II), 'Vienna Medical School' (Chapter II), and 'Femininity' (Chapter VIII). About half of Chapter IV, 'A Newspaper and its Antagonist', is also missing. It is clear from the emendations to the table of contents, which are in Wittels's handwriting, that Wittels was dissatisfied with the book in its original form and intended to alter or omit certain chapters. The text of the Introduction by Fritz Wittels derives from a further five-page typescript entitled 'From the draft of an introduction to an unfinished autobiography', which appears to have been retyped after Wittels's death.

The second main source is a planned volume of more general reminiscences, which was to be entitled 'When Vienna was Vienna: Reminiscences of a Former Resident'. The list of contents which Wittels drafted by hand for this second volume (Fig. 48) shows that it would have included chapters on his work at the Vienna Cottage Hospital and his experiences during the First World War. It seems likely that three chapters in a larger typeface, which

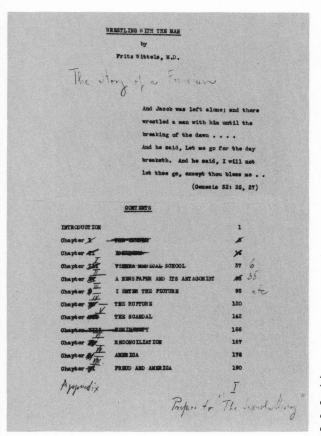

47. 'Wrestling with the Man: The Story of a Freudian': facsimile of original title page and table of contents, with handwritten emendations by Wittels.

contain further information about Wittels's early life, derive from this 'When Vienna was Vienna' typescript: an untitled chapter with pages numbered 1–22, probably 'Roots' (Chapter I); a second untitled chapter with pages numbered 1–20, probably 'Attachment' (Chapter II); and Chapter III (pages 1–25), with the hand-written title 'Detachment'. In these three draft chapters Irma Karczewska, the 'child woman', is referred to as Mitzerl, whereas in the 'Wrestling with the Man' typescript she is known as Mitzi. Sections from these three additional chapters, including the whole account of the Vienna Medical School, have been incorporated in the present edition of the memoirs, since they serve to amplify the main narrative. And Karczewska's original name, Irma, has been restored throughout.

Wittels did not simply abandon the 'When Vienna Was Vienna' project, but rather decided to transpose it into an autobiographical novel with the same title. This forms a further substantial typescript, written in the style of a novella, which survives in the Brill Library. Since this takes the form of a third-person fictional

When
Vienna
was
Vienna

Reminiscences of a former Resident

or: _Vienna Bijou_
or: Vienna to be mentioned in the subtitle only
or: Tales from the Vienna Woods

Fritz Wittels, M. D.

C. C. WILKENING & SON, INC.
40 East 51st Street
New York City.

48. 'When Vienna Was Vienna':
facsimile of original title page and table
of contents, handwritten by Wittels.

I. The Roots
II. Attachment
III. Detachment
IV. Music of all kind
V. A Private Hospital : Day
VI. A Private Hospital : Night
VII. Famous Friends and enemies
VIII. The War : Front in Russia — in Italy
IX. Hinterland
X. Auxiliaries to Turkey : Constpl. — Aleppo — Damascus — Jerusalem —
        The Ligro river
XI. Armistice — Homecoming — The city after the war
XII. A Viennese in America

narrative, it has no direct bearing on the memoirs. The further typescripts which survive among the Wittels papers include the German manuscript of a play, 'Die Nixen', dated 1897; fifteen chapters for a book to be entitled 'Phantom Psychology'; the final typescript of 'Universal Subsistence Army' (an exposition of the ideas of the Austrian social reformer Joseph Popper-Lynkeus); and the complete typescript of 'Germany is Curable' (a study of the historical origins of Nazi phobias about sexuality). There is also a five-page memo by Wittels, dated 13 March 1940, criticizing Karen Horney's deviations from orthodox Freudian theory; and various other letters and notebooks, some of which date back to Wittels's experiences in Vienna.

The Wittels papers, taken together with his many publications in both English and German, provide one of the richest sources for the study of Austrian culture in the early twentieth century and the evolution of psychoanalysis both in Vienna and in New York. A systematic reassessment of his life and work is long overdue.

C. Publications by Fritz Wittels

Abbreviations

References to the magazine *Die Fackel*, ed. Karl Kraus (Vienna, 1899–1936) are identified by the letter *F*, followed by the issue and page number.

The *Minutes of the Vienna Psychoanalytic Society*, translated by M. Nunberg, ed. Herman Nunberg and Ernst Federn, 4 vols (New York, 1962–75) are identified as *Minutes*, followed by volume and page number.

The Standard Edition of the Complete Psychological Works of Sigmund Freud, translated from the German under the general editorship of James Strachey, 24 vols (London, 1966–74) is identified as *SE*, followed by volume and page number.

Notebook: During the final years of her life, from October 1930 onwards, Irma Karczewska (Wittels's 'child woman') recorded personal reminiscences and reflections about her twenty-five-year relationship with Karl Kraus in a series of dated entries, handwritten in pencil, in a school exercise book, now in a private collection in Vienna. In this notebook, which is cited from a typewritten transcript, she engages Kraus in an impassioned imaginary dialogue, addressing him as 'du' (the intimate second-

person singular pronoun). References to this source are identified as
Notebook (followed by the date).

Books and booklets (in German and English)

Der Taufjude, Vienna, 1904
Die sexuelle Not, Vienna, 1909
Alte Liebeshändel, Vienna, 1909
Ezechiel, der Zugereiste, Berlin, 1910
Tragische Motive: Das Unbewußte von Held und Heldin, Berlin, 1911
Alles um Liebe: Eine Urweltdichtung, Berlin, 1912
Der Juwelier von Bagdad, Berlin, 1914 (*The Jeweller of Bagdad*, New
    York, 1927)
Über den Tod und über den Glauben an Gott: Zwei Vorträge, Vienna,
    1914
Die Vernichtung der Not, Vienna, 1922 (*An End to Poverty*, London,
    1925)
Zacharias Pamperl, oder der verschobene Halbmond, Vienna, 1923
Sigmund Freud: Der Mann, die Lehre, die Schule, Vienna, 1924
    (*Sigmund Freud: His Personality, His Teaching and his School*,
    London, 1924)
Wunderbare Heilungen, Leipzig and Vienna, 1925
Die Technik der Psychoanalyse, Munich, 1926
Die Befreiung des Kindes, Stuttgart, 1927 (*Set the Children Free!*,
    London, 1932)
Die Psychoanalyse: Neue Wege der Seelenkunde, Vienna, 1927
Die Welt ohne Zuchthaus, Berne, 1928
Critique of Love, New York, 1929
*Freud and his Time: The Influence of the Master Psychologist on the
    Emotional Problems in Our Lives*, New York, 1931
Interpreting Your Dreams, New York (Home Information Booklets),
    1936
Sex Habits of American Women, New York, 1951

Contributions to the Vienna Psychoanalytic Society

'Tatjana Leontiev' (10 April 1907; *Minutes*, I, 160–65)
'Female Physicians' (15 May 1907; *Minutes*, I, 195–201)
'The Great Courtesan' (29 May 1907; *Minutes*, I, 195, footnote)

'Venereal Disease' (13 November 1907; *Minutes*, I, 238–41)

'The Normal Psychiatrist' (22 January 1908; *Minutes*, I, 286–7)

'The Natural Position of Women' (11 March 1908; *Minutes*, I, 437–54)

'Sexual Perversity' (18 November 1908; *Minutes*, II, 53–64)

Discussion of Wittels's book *Die sexuelle Not* (16 December 1908; *Minutes*, II, 82–92)

'Analysis of a Hysterical State of Confusion' (27 October 1909; *Minutes*, II, 282–9)

'The "Fackel"-Neurosis' (12 January 1910; *Minutes*, II, 382–93)

Short stories and articles in 'Die Fackel'

(FW) = published under the name of Fritz Wittels; (A) = published under the pseudonym Avicenna; (FW/A) indicates that both names are given: Dr Fritz Wittels (Avicenna).

'Ladislaus Posthumus' (FW), February 1907 (*F*, 218, 14–20)

'Das größte Verbrechen des Strafgesetzes' (A), February 1907 (*F*, 219–20, 1–22)

'Die drei Schwestern' (FW), March 1907 (*F*, 221, 11–15)

'Das Stammbuch' (FW), March 1907 (*F*, 222, 5–12)

'Weibliche Ärzte' (A), May 1907 (*F*, 225, 10–24)

'Die vermeyntliche Hexe' (FW), June 1907 (*F*, 227–8, 26–34)

'Das Kindweib' (A), July 1907 (*F*, 230–31, 14–33)

'Die Lustseuche' (A), December 1907 (*F*, 238, 1–24)

'Die Versuchung des jungen Prenberger' (FW), February 1908 (*F*, 244, 11–20)

'Weibliche Attentäter' (FW/A) March 1908 (*F*, 246–7, 26–38)

'Die Feministen' (FW), March 1908 (*F*, 248, 9–14)

'Sexuelle Aufklärung' (FW), April 1908 (*F*, 250, 16–21)

'Gottesurteil' (FW), May 1908 (*F*, 254–5, 14–19)

Note: None of these stories or articles is available in English, although a radically revised version of Wittels's theory of the 'child woman' is included in his book *Critique of Love* (1929).

Articles in German in other journals

Before he emigrated to America, Wittels contributed numerous articles on cultural and political subjects to German and Austrian magazines and newspapers, including the *Berliner Tageblatt* (1908), the Munich magazine *März* (1908), the Berlin theatre magazine *Die Schaubühne* (1911) and the progressive Viennese newspaper *Der Abend* (1919). During the 1920s and 1930s he also contributed to educational and psychoanalytic journals, including *Zeitschrift für Psychoanalytische Pädagogik* (1926–7), *Almanach des Internationalen Psychoanalytischen Verlags* (1928–9), *Neue Erziehung* (1928), *Die Psychoanalytische Bewegung* (1929–33), *Imago* (1934) and *Internationale Zeitschrift für Psychoanalyse* (1934–37).

Articles in English

The range of Wittels's interests during his career in the United States is reflected in his many contributions to psychoanalytic journals and other educational publications:

'Some Remarks on Kleptomania', *Journal of Nervous and Mental Disease*, 69 (1929), 214–51.

'The Lilith Neurosis', *Psychoanalytical Review*, 19 (1932), 241–56.

'Revision of a Biography', *Psychoanalytical Review*, 20 (1933), 361–74.

'Psychoanalysis and Literature', in *Psychoanalysis Today*, ed. Sandor Lorand (New York, 1933), 338–48.

'Revision of a Biography', *American Journal of Psychology*, 45 (1933), 745–9.

'The Superego in our Judgments of Sex', *International Journal of Psychoanalysis*, 14 (1933), 335–40.

'Mona Lisa and Feminine Beauty: A Study in Bisexuality', *International Journal of Psychoanalysis*, 15 (1934), 25–40.

'Motherhood and Bisexuality', *Psychoanalytical Review*, 21 (1934), 180–93.

'Masculine and Feminine in Three Psychic Systems', *Psychoanalytical Review*, 22 (1935), 409–23.

'A Type of Woman with a Three-fold Love Life', *International Journal of Psychoanalysis*, 16 (1935), 462–73.

'The Criminal Psychopath in the Psychoanalytic System', *Psychoanalytical Review*, 24 (1937), 276–91.

'The Mystery of Masochism', *Psychoanalytical Review*, 24 (1937), 139–49.

'The Phenomenon of Transference in a Case of Phobia', *Journal of Nervous and Mental Disease*, 88 (1938), 12–17.

'The Position of the Psychopath in the Psychoanalytic System',

International Journal of Psychoanalysis, 19 (1938), 471–88.

'The Neo-Adlerians', *American Journal of Sociology*, 45 (1939), 433–45.

'Unconscious Phantoms in Neurotics', *Psychoanalytic Quarterly*, 8 (1939), 141–63.

'Phantom Formation in a Case of Epilepsy', *Psychoanalytic Quarterly*, 9 (1940), 98–108.

'Psychology and Treatment of Depersonalization', *Psychoanalytical Review*, 27 (1940), 57–64.

'In Memoriam: Paul Schilder', *Psychoanalytic Quarterly*, 10 (1941), 131–4.

'The Phantom of Omnipotence', *Psychoanalytical Review*, 28 (1941), 163–72.

'Kleptomania and Other Psychopathic Crimes', *Journal of Criminal Psychopathology*, 4 (1942), 205–16.

'Struggles of a Homosexual in Pre-Hitler Germany', *Journal of Criminal Psychopathology*, 4 (1943), 408–23.

'Collective Defense Mechanisms against Homosexuality', *Psychoanalytical Review*, 31 (1944), 19–33.

'Freud's Scientific Cradle', *American Journal of Psychiatry*, 100 (1944), 521–8.

'In Memoriam: Albert Joseph Storfer', *Psychoanalytic Quarterly*, 14 (1945), 234–5.

'The Contribution of Benjamin Rush to Psychiatry', *Bulletin of the History of Medicine*, 20 (1946), 157–66.

'Economic and Psychological Historiography', *American Journal of Sociology*, 51 (1946), 527–32.

'Psychoanalysis and History: The Nibelungs and the Bible', *Psychoanalytic Quarterly*, 15 (1946), 88–103.

'Freud's Correlation with Joseph Popper-Lynkeus', *Psychoanalytical Review*, 36 (1947), 492–7.

'Brill – the Pioneer', *Psychoanalytical Review*, 35 (1948), 394–8.

'The Ego of the Adolescent', in *Searchlights on Delinquency*, ed. Kurt R. Eissler (New York, 1949), 256–62.

'Homosexuality', in *Encyclopedia of Criminology*, ed. Vernon C. Branham and Samuel B. Kutash (New York, 1949), 190–94.

'A Neglected Boundary of Psychoanalysis', *Psychoanalytic Quarterly*, 19 (1949), 44–59.

'The Spirit of Psychoanalysis', *Psychoanalytical Review*, 26 (1949), 240–54.

D. NOTES ON THE TEXT

Editor's Preface

1. In his book *Freud : A Life for our Time* (London, 1988), published two
    years after the conversation recorded in this Preface, Peter Gay
    specifically refers to the typescript of Wittels's unpublished memoirs
    (p. 214, footnote).

Introduction by Fritz Wittels: Wrestling with the Man

1. The concept of ambivalence was introduced by Ernst Bleuler in a
    lecture delivered in Berne in 1910, 'Vortrag über Ambivalenz',
    reported in *Zentralblatt für Psychoanalyse*, (1911), 1, 266. Freud
    himself takes up 'the excellent term "ambivalence"' in 'The Dyn-
    amics of Transference' (1912), *SE*, 12, 106.
2. Shakespeare, *Hamlet*, Act II, scene i.
3. Schnitzler's diaries contain numerous references to Wittels, whom he
    first met on 24 September 1910. While on leave from military
    service, Wittels paid him a number of visits, during one of which the
    normally sceptical Schnitzler admitted to strong but unsentimental
    feelings for his Austrian homeland: 'Mein Heimatsgefühl – außerhalb
    alles intellectualen und sentimentalen'. See Arthur Schnitzler,
    Tagebuch 1913–1916 (Vienna, 1983), p. 273: entry for 12 March 1916.

1: Childhood in Vienna

1. Charlotte Wittels, née Fuchs, was born on 12 November 1852 in
    Galicia (now Ukraine), the daughter of Chaje and David Fuchs, a
    tenant farmer. On 13 February 1873 she married Rubin Wittels in
    Vienna and became the mother of five children (Toni, Otto,
    Maximilian, Siegfried [Fritz] and Emerich). She died on 11 January
    1887 of peritonitis and is buried in the Jewish Section of the Vienna
    Central Cemetry (Zentralfriedhof).
2. Sigmund Freud, 'Leonardo da Vinci and a Memory of his
    Childhood' (1910), *SE*, 11, 63–137.
3. The Frau Schreiber sequence, which forms part of the draft chapters
    for 'When Vienna was Vienna', has at this point been been conflated
    with the first section of 'Wrestling with the Man', in order to form a
    more balanced opening chapter.
4. Nestroy, *Einen Jux will er sich machen*, Act III, scene iv:

    > *Fräulein Blumenblatt*:   Auch ich habe einst geliebt.
    > *Christoph*:   Das kann ich mir denken.
    > *Fräulein Blumenblatt*:   Und der Mann der mich liebte –
    > *Weinberl*:   Das kann ich mir nicht denken –

5. The author's father Rubin (Rudolph) Feiwisch Wittels was born in Galicia on 1 January 1849. At the time of his marriage to his first wife, Charlotte Fuchs, he was living at Leopoldsgasse No. 8 in Vienna's Second District (the Leopoldstadt), and his marriage certificate gives his profession as Broker in the Exchange Market. After his first wife's death he married on 11 March 1888 Malke Sadger, sister of the Isidor Sadger (a physician who later made his name as a psychoanalyst). There were two children by this second marriage, Grete and Mitzi.

6. The Burgtheater playbill for 1 November 1888 confirms that Fritz Krastel did indeed play the noble brigand Jaromir. However, the role of the Ancestress was *not* played by Charlotte Wolter, as Wittels mistakenly recalls, but by Anna Bauer. There is no record in the archives of the Österreichisches Theatermuseum that Wolter ever played this role.

7. 'In the natural progress of occurrences' ('Im Verlauf der Begebenheiten . . .') was a favourite phrase used by the locksmith Gluthammer in Nestroy, *Der Zerissene*, Act I, scene iii.

8. A free translation (perhaps from memory) of the following lines from Act III of Grillparzer's *Die Ahnfrau* (1816): 'Ja, ich bins, du Unglückselge, / Ja, ich bins, den du genannt; / Bins, den jene Wälder kennen, / Bins, den Mörder Bruder nennen, / Bin der Räuber Jaromir!'

9. The final words spoken by the Ancestress at the end of Act V of *Die Ahnfrau*: 'Öffne dich, du stille Klause, / Denn die Ahnfrau kehrt nach Hause.'

10. This phrase, frequently attributed to Nestroy himself, is in fact spoken by one of his characters, Fabian Strick in *Die beiden Nachtwandler*, Act I, scene xvi: 'Ich glaube von jedem Menschen das Schlechteste, selbst von mir, und ich hab' mich noch selten getäuscht'.

11. A phrase used by the millionaire Goldfuchs in Nestroy's *Zu ebener Erde und erster Stock*, Act II, scene viii: 'Eine Million ist eine schußfeste Brustwehr, über welche man stolz hinabblickt, wenn die Truppen des Schicksals heranstürmen.'

12. From a monologue spoken by Gottlieb Herb in Nestroy's *Der Schützling*, Act IV, scene x: 'Überhaupt hat der Fortschritt das an sich, daß er viel größer ausschaut, als er wirklich ist.'

13. From the speech by the revolutionary Ultra in Nestroy's *Freiheit in Krähwinkel*, Act I, scene xiv: 'Ein Censor ist ein menschgewordener Bleistift oder ein Bleistift gewordener Mensch; ein fleischgewordener Strich über die Erzeugnisse des Geistes, ein Krokodil, das an den Ufern des Ideenstromes lagert und den darin schwimmenden Dichtern die Köpf abbeißt.'

14. The original German of the passages quoted from Nestroy's *Judith und Holofernes* reads as follows: '*Holofernes*: Ich bin der Glanzpunkt der Natur [. . .] Ich möcht' mich einmal mit mir selbst zusammenhetzen, nur um zu sehen, wer der Stärkere ist, ich oder

ich. [. . .] Laß aber erst das Zelt ordentlich zusammenräumen, überall liegen Erstochene herum' (scene iii); '*Hosea*: Das Herumkommandieren fangt an mich zu verdrießen. *Nabal*: Is er mehr als wir? *Ammon*: Is nicht ein Jud als wie der andere? [. . .] *Assad*: Links g'schaut! *Hosea*: Warum? Links is gar nix! Warum sollen wir schauen links? Was ist da zu sehn?' (scene xvii); '*Joab*: Ihr habt einen Feldherrn ohne Kopf!' (scene xxiv).

15.　Wittels, like Freud, was a great admirer of the Austrian social reformer Popper-Lynkeus (1838–1921). Their earliest contacts date from before the First World War, and from 1919 onwards Wittels became an active campaigner for Popper's form of enlightened state socialism, first in articles written for the Viennese newspaper *Der Abend*, later through his book *Die Vernichtung der Not* (*An End to Poverty*). Towards the end of his life Wittels drafted a further exposition of Popper's ideas under the title 'Universal Subsistence Army' (unpublished typescript in the Brill Library, New York).

16.　Wittels first visited New York in 1928, after receiving an invitation to deliver lectures at the New School for Social Research. He was also invited to give lectures by the New York Psychoanalytic Society, of which he became a member by transfer from Vienna in March 1932. After establishing himself as an analyst in New York, he lived at 91 Central Park West, where he had an office on the ground floor.

17.　The pretext for the massacre of 1421 was provided by a court case in which a Christian woman confessed to allowing the holy sacraments to be desecrated by Jews in the provincial town of Enns. Approximately 2,000 Jews in Upper and Lower Austria were imprisoned during the summer of 1420, some of whom were subsequently deported and found sanctuary in Hungary. Many more died in prison or committed suicide, rather than submit to enforced baptism. Finally, on 12 March 1421, a total of 210 Jews were burnt to death at Erdberg near Vienna.

　　Since all Jewish houses and property in Vienna were confiscated by Albrecht V, historians have identified economic envy as the primary motive behind the pogrom. See Ignaz Schwarz, *Das Wiener Ghetto, seine Häuser und seine Bewohner* (Quellen und Forschungen zur Geschichte der Juden in Deutschösterreich, Vienna, 1909). For Austrian Nazis, however, the expulsion and massacre of 1421, which was followed by a second enforced exodus in 1670, provided a historical precedent for the systematic persecution of the Jews after the Anschluss. See Robert Körber, *Rassesieg in Wien, der Grenzfeste des Reiches: 1421–1670–1938* (Vienna, 1939).

　　The monument on the Judenplatz implies that the Jews themselves were to blame for the massacre because of their refusal to accept baptism. The Latin inscription reads as follows: 'Through the waters of Jordan bodies are cleansed of pestilence and evil; and all hidden sinfulness is washed away. Hence the wrath spreads fiercely through the whole city, chastizing the Jewish dogs in 1421 for their terrible crimes. The world is now purified through Deucalion's flood and in the burning fiery furnace they atone for their sins.'

18. Wittels is being ironic about the National Socialist myth that Jesus was of 'Aryan' descent. He himself came from an assimilated Jewish family and criticized those who converted to Christianity for opportunistic reasons in one of his earliest writings, *Der Taufjude* (The Baptised Jew), a forty-page pamphlet published in 1904.

19. The original table of contents for 'Wrestling with the Man' included 'Chapter II: IDEALISM', presumably dealing with Wittels's schooldays. This chapter appears to have been lost or destroyed, but autobiographical passages in his other writings suggest that he found the Austrian school system oppressive.

2: Freud and the Vienna Medical School

1. According to the account of 'therapeutic nihilism' given in William M. Johnston's *The Austrian Mind: An Intellectual and Social History 1848–1938* (Chapter 15), the conception of medicine which developed in Vienna during the nineteenth century placed the main emphasis on advanced techniques of scientific diagnosis. The therapeutic aim of actually curing patients tended to be seen as secondary, since the available methods of treatment were manifestly so primitive.

2. 'Kinderlähmung' is the title of an unsigned article on infantile paralysis, almost certainly by Freud, which appeared in *Handwörterbuch der gesamten Medizin*, Vol. 2 (Stuttgart, 1891), edited by A. Villaret (*not* by Nothnagel). Freud's early study of speech disorders appeared under the title *Zur Auffassung der Aphasien* (Vienna, 1891).

3. 'Die Geister regen sich, es ist eine Lust zu leben', letter of 25 October 1518 from Ulrich von Hutten to the Nuremberg humanist Willibald Pirckheimer.

4. In October 1923 Freud underwent an operation to remove a cancerous growth from his jaw, and in consequence he had to wear a prothesis which affected his speech.

5. These stories appeared in *Die Fackel* on 27 March 1907 ('Das Stammbuch', *F*, 222, 5–12) and 5 February 1907 ('Ladislaus Posthumus', *F*, 218, 14–20).

3: Kraus and the Neue Freie Presse

1. Wittels set out his theory of Kraus's father complex in a paper delivered to the Vienna Psychoanalytic Society on 12 January 1910 under the title 'The "Fackel"-Neurosis' (*Minutes*, II, 382–93). Although this was one of the most controversial of his early contributions to psychoanalysis, Wittels alludes to it only obliquely

in his memoirs. His rather convoluted argument has been sum-marized as follows:

> Wittels starts from the assumption that 'pathographies of artists' show 'how art and neurosis are related, and how the one passes over into the other'. The first problem is to identify the 'personal motive' which led Kraus to launch a bitter attack on journalism, especially the *Neue Freie Presse* and the Jewish community it served. The answer came to Wittels when he 'had a vision in which he saw his own father reading the *Neue Freie Presse*'. It dawned on him that the *Neue Freie Presse* is 'the father's paper', perhaps even 'the father's organ', against which Kraus directs his own 'small organ', *Die Fackel*. Moriz Benedikt is thus attacked as a father figure. This is corroborated by the fact that Kraus's father was named Jacob, meaning 'the blessed one' – Benedictus. 'From all this [Wittels concludes] it is evident that it was a *neurotic* attitude towards one particular newspaper that was the starting point of his hatred for journalists. [. . .] In order to understand this neurotic hatred of his, one need only remember that the origin and starting point of every neurosis is the Oedipus motif.'
>
> In the second period of *Die Fackel* (Wittels continues), when Kraus deals with the problem of sexuality, 'his private neurosis has become linked with the general neurosis of the time.' He has thus 'lived through much of what Freud has found out by way of scientific work, and has presented it in an artistic form'. This change of direction may be connected with the death of an actress (Annie Kalmar). Even though this phase of *Die Fackel* is an artistic achievement, 'in a few instances the fundamental neurotic scheme betrays itself'. This is particularly evident in Kraus's view that, except for the woman who gives herself to everyone, 'all women are hysterical'. This may be interpreted in Freudian terms as 'the reversal of a previous overvaluing of the mother and being disappointed in that love'. Wittels adds that in later years 'Kraus had in fact such a wretched attitude towards his mother that his brothers were able to put the blame on him for her death'. The third phase of *Die Fackel*, after Kraus's break with Wittels, is 'the period of artistic sterility'. Kraus 'first sexualized the newspaper, [. . .] now it is *form* that he sexualizes' – the form of the aphorism. In his concluding remarks Wittels touches on 'the problem of the satirist': 'Kraus is a misshapen man, as was Voltaire', but 'differs from Voltaire in the inconsequentiality of his accomplishments'. Kraus's great 'dramatic-parodistic talent' may also be a factor.
> (Edward Timms, *Karl Kraus – Apocalyptic Satirist*, London and New Haven, 1986, p. 101)

The treatment of Kraus's personality in this paper and its reception by other members of the Psychoanalytic Society have been described by Thomas Szasz in *Karl Kraus and the Soul Doctors* (London, 1977) as a 'psychoanalytic lynching party' (p. 34). Actually, Wittels's paper met with a mixed response. Viktor Tausk questioned whether his 'scientific' approach was adequate to the task of 'illuminating a personality', while Freud himself expressed serious reservations in his summing up of the discussion: 'Some of the points Wittels adduced are undoubtedly correct: the father complex, the character of the milieu, Jewishness, the return of enmities as neurotic character, etc. But we forget too easily that we have no right to place neurosis in the foreground, wherever a great accomplishment is concerned' (*Minutes*, II, 388 and 391).

2. Wittels is here conflating two different hoaxes, the first relating to the earthquake, concocted by Kraus in February 1908 ('Das Erdbeben', *F*, 245, 16–24); the second about the 'mining–dog', planted in the *Neue Freie Presse* in November 1911 by a reader of *Die Fackel* named Arthur Schütz ('Der Grubenhund', *F*, 336–7, 5–9).

3. The opening words of Kraus's anti-Nazi polemic *Dritte Walpurgisnacht*, written in 1933 but not published as a whole until 1952. Wittels is quoting from an excerpt which appeared in *Die Fackel* in July 1934 ('Mir fällt zu Hitler nichts ein'; *F*, 890–905, 153).

4: Spiritual Fathers

1. The original letter from Kraus to Wittels, reproduced in facsimile as Figure 15, has generously been made available for publication by John R. Wittels.

2. 'Das größte Verbrechen des Strafgesetzes', published in *Die Fackel* on 22 February 1907 (*F*, 219–20, 1–22).

3. 'Weibliche Ärzte', published in *Die Fackel* on 3 May 1907 (*F*, 225, 10–24).

4. *Sigmund Freud: His Personality, His Teaching and His School* (1924).

5. The article 'Weibliche Ärzte' was indeed severely criticized at the meeting of the Vienna Psychoanalytic Society on 15 May 1907. Freud himself, after initially expressing 'appreciation for an original, high-spirited, ingenious essay', actually concluded that Wittels's point of view was 'juvenile', although he agreed that 'women cannot equal man's achievement in the sublimation of sexuality' (*Minutes*, I, 195–201).

6. Ludwig von Janikowski was one of Kraus's closest friends in the period 1904–9. After Janikowski's death in July 1911, Kraus paid tribute to him in an eloquent obituary notice (*F*, 331–2, 64).

7. The essayist Karl Hauer was one of the most prominent contributors to *Die Fackel* during the years 1905 to 1909, writing numerous articles about eroticism and art.

8. Irma Karczewska (1890–1933).

According to records of the City of Vienna (Wiener Stadt- und Landesarchiv), she was born on 30 January 1890. This date of birth confirms Wittels's statement that she was only seventeen when he first met her in 1907. Irma, who is also sometimes known as Maria, must therefore have been barely fifteen when she appeared on stage in Kraus's production of Wedekind's *Die Büchse der Pandora* on 29 May 1905. It has not been possible to document Karczewska's subsequent stage career, although in May 1906 Kraus praised her contribution to the Viennese cabaret 'Nachtlicht', referring to her by her stage name Ingrid Loris (*F*, 203, 19). Another of her stage names was Irma Kardinger. She subsequently changed her surname and her religion, presumably in connection with her marriages (she appears to have married four times). Her foray into the Berlin theatre around 1910 was certainly unsuccessful, although her notebook records that she coached Kraus on stage technique in preparation for his first public readings in Berlin in January 1910. In 1912 she is again recorded as resident in Vienna, under the name Maria Haselhoff-Lich, and her religion is given as Roman Catholic. By that date she had already separated from her first husband Haselhoff, an Austrian industrialist. During the First World War she was married again, to an engineer named Friese, and it appears from her notebooks that she may also have had a third husband named Benedicter. After the war she finally married Georg Christoduloff from Tatar Pazardjik in Bulgaria, changing her religion to Greek Orthodox. Her notebook also records that she lived with a man named Henri Triadou, whom she cared for until his death in 1926. Her own death on 1 January 1933 is registered under the name Maria Christoduloff, in an entry which again gives her date of birth as 30 January 1890.

Irma Karczewska's date of birth has, however, been questioned by another researcher, Sophie Schick, who argues that it was common for actresses to have their birthdate re-registered, so as to give the impression of being younger than they really were. It is thus conceivable that Karczewska, who had other sexual partners before she met Kraus, was born earlier than 1890. However, she herself repeatedly claims in her reminiscences that she was only fifteen when they first met. At one point she even recalls that Kraus, whom she addresses in the second person, 'took me away from home as a girl of fourteen-and-a-half' ('mich als 14½ jähriges Mädchen vom Haus wegnahmst', *Notebook*, 12 October 1930, underlined by Karczewska).

9.   The cult of the 'courtesan' ('Hetäre') was actually launched in *Die Fackel* by Karl Hauer, in an article of November 1905 entitled 'Lob der Hetäre', published under the pseudonym Lucianus (*F*, 188, 11–14). His choice of pseudonym was probably inspired by the work of the Greek satirist Lucian, author of *Conversations of the Courtesans* (in German: *Hetärengespräche*).

5:   The Child Woman

1.   In letters written by members of Kraus's circle, for example the author Erich Mühsam and the actress Kete Parsenow, Irma

Karczewska is characteristically referred to as 'die Kleine' ('the little one'), a reflection on her shortness of stature as well as her tender years.

2. This statement must be modified in the light of comments in Karczewska's notebook. Kraus did indeed contribute intermittently to her finances over a period of about twenty-five years, continuing to support her after their personal relationship finally came to an end in the mid-1920s. He also made provision in his will for her grave to be tended after his own death: 'das Grab der armen Frau Maria Christoduloff'. However, Karczewska records that in August 1929 she received a final settlement from Kraus through his lawyer Oskar Samek, on condition that she surrendered any further claims – a transaction which she later regretted, since she felt that Kraus was committed to supporting her financially for life (*Notebook*, 12 October 1930). During the following years the *Notebook* is filled with complaints about her financial difficulties and expressions of her grief at having lost Kraus's affections.

3. There is no evidence that her first husband actually was Swedish. On the first page of the *Notebook* the names of her husbands are listed as Haseloff, Friese, Benedicter and Christoduloff.

4. The strength of this infatuation is reflected in a series of eight handwritten love letters from Fritz Wittels to Irma Karczewska, addressed to 'Liebes Irmerl' and dated between April and December 1907, now in the manuscript collection of the Vienna City Library.

5. 'Das Kindweib', published in *Die Fackel* on 15 July 1907 (*F*, 230–31, 14–33). This is evidently a revised version of the paper originally presented to the Vienna Psychoanalytic Society on 29 May 1907 under the title 'The Great Courtesan' ('Die große Hetäre', *Minutes*, I, 195, footnote). There is no record in the *Minutes* either of the contents of this paper or the ensuing discussion, and it may well be that the subject – the cult of precocious and totally uninhibited female sexuality – was regarded as too scandalous to be included in the stenographic record of 'Scientific Meetings'.

6. In 'Das Kindweib' Wittels refers to Freud's 'Sexualtheorie' (*F*, 230–31, 16), that is, to the account of 'infantile sexuality' and 'sensual sucking' developed in the second of Freud's *Three Essays on the Theory of Sexuality* (1905; *SE*, 7, 179–83).

7. Circumstantial evidence suggests that the editors of the *Minutes* conflated elements from the suppressed stenographic record of the discussion of 'The Great Courtesan' ('Die große Hetäre', 29 May 1907) with the published record of the discussion of Wittels's paper on 'Female Physicians', presented a fortnight earlier (15 May). In response to the paper on 'Female Physicians' Freud is recorded as saying: 'The ideal of the courtesan [*Hetäre*] has no place in our culture. [. . .] A woman who, like the courtesan, is not trustworthy in sexuality is altogether worthless. She is simply a *Haderlump* [a ragamuffin].' (*Minutes*, I, 200.) Since there is no reference to the cult of the 'Hetäre' in Wittels's article on 'Female Physicians', Freud must

be referring to Wittels's subsequent paper on 'Die große Hetäre'. The same presumably applies to Wittels's reaction, also misleadingly recorded as a reaction to discussion of 'Female Physicians': 'Wittels feels so shaken by a word of Freud's (the courtesan is a *Haderlump*) that at the moment he cannot answer the objections in detail' (*Minutes*, I, 201). However, when Wittels published his eulogy to the 'Hetäre' in *Die Fackel* under the title 'Das Kindweib' six weeks later, he acknowledged (without mentioning Freud by name) that some people might regard the polygamous primal woman as a 'Haderlump' (*F*, 230–31, 20).

8. Even in its amended form, as published in *Die Fackel*, 'Das Kindweib' can certainly not be taken seriously as a contribution to psychology. The idealization of the 'Hetäre' is too obviously coloured by turn-of-the-century erotic cults and fantasies, as is evident from the repeated references to Kraus and Wedekind. Wittels also cites as one of his authorities the *Hetärengespräche* of Lucian (which had just been published in a new German translation embellished with erotic drawings by Gustav Klimt). It is nevertheless clear from a letter written to Irma dated 21 July 1907 that Wittels expected her to feel flattered by his projection of her personality: 'Hast Du nun "das Kindweib" durchgesehn? Alle Leute fragen mich nach dem Modell dazu, denn auch denen der Artikel nicht so gefällt sind begierig das Urbild dazu kennen zu lernen. Sie merken, daß an dem Urbild was dran sein muß' ('Have you looked through "The Childwoman"? Everyone's asking me about the model for it, since even those who are not so taken by the article are curious to get to know the original. They realize that the original must be quite something.') Looking back on her experiences later in life, Irma Karczewska did indeed express a certain pride at having become known among members of Kraus's circle as a 'literary-historical personality' ('literarhistorische Persönlichkeit', *Notebook*, 30 January 1930).

9. Freud's essay 'On Narcissism: An Introduction' appeared in 1914. In suggesting that Freud was influenced by the concept of the 'child woman', Wittels is probably thinking of the passage about 'the great charm of narcissistic women' (*SE*, 14, 89). Further echoes of the Kraus-Wittels-Irma Karczewska affair may be detected in Freud's essay of 1910, 'A Special Type of Choice of Object Made by Men', which refers to the 'triangular situation' in which two men may be in love with the same 'openly promiscuous' woman, without necessarily experiencing any jealousy (*SE*, 11, 166–7).

10. Wittels invited Irma Karczewska to accompany him to Venice in a letter dated 9 September 1907, written from Bad Ischl, where he was holidaying with Kraus. Since this letter gives a vivid impression of Wittels's feelings for Irma at the time, as well as forming an ironic counterpoint to what actually occurred in Venice, the full text is reproduced here, preceded by an English translation:

   Dear dear little Irma! Even if you now sort things out in

Vienna, you still surely can't stay in Vienna. Quite apart from the measles epidemic I really don't know what you would do there, with everyone away and no possibility of study or entertainment starting before October. If you agree, let's go together on Saturday or Sunday to Venice. We leave in the evening, next morning we're there. We'll find a splendid place to stay, for we'll bathe in the sea at the Lido [and see] theatres, paintings, beautiful churches. Venice is really like a fairy-tale, and we'll make love if you want to, or not if you don't want to. Kraus will join us for a day or two, he is longing for you, I have given him your loving and kind messages, just as he deserves, we talk about you all day [.] We'll stay away for 10–14 days. By the way, the picture of you in profile is even more beautiful than the one I've got, if that were possible, one can't look at it without kissing it. You'll hardly be able to answer this letter, for by Wednesday or Thursday lunchtime we'll be meeting in the Mühlgasse. I don't dare to show the warmth of my feelings to you, not even in a letter. Since in reality you don't want it at the moment and I can see you before my very eyes as I write to you, I must restrain myself. But you must believe that I have the sweetest dreams, even while I'm awake, I am lying at your feet and embracing your knees, I'm caressing your brown skin in private places and I am fantastically happy that I'm so fond of you and you too are a bit fond of me and are so good to me.

Affectionate kisses from your Fritz.

Liebes liebes Irmerl! Wenn Du jetzt in Wien in Ordnung kommst, kannst Du doch noch nicht in Wien bleiben. Abgesehen von der Blatterepidemie wüßte ich wirklich nicht, was Du da machen sollst, wo noch niemand ist und weder Studium noch Vergnügen vor Oktober beginnen kann. Wenn es Dir recht ist fahren wir Samstag oder Sonntag zusammen nach Venedig. Abends fahren wir weg, andern Morgen sind wir da. Wir werden prachtvoll wohnen, wenn [*sic*] wir wollen am Lido im Meer baden, Theater, Bilder, schöne Kirchen; Venedig ist in der Tat wie ein Märchen und wir werden uns lieben, wenn Du willst, und nicht, wenn Du nicht willst. Kraus kommt für einen oder zwei Tage hin, er sehnt sich sehr nach Dir, ich habe ihm alles Liebe und Gute von Dir ausgerichtet, wie er es verdient, wir sprechen den ganzen Tag von Dir, 10–14 Tage würden wir ausbleiben. Du, das Bild im Profil ist womöglich noch schöner als das meine, man kann es nicht ansehen ohne es zu küssen. Antworten wirst Du auf diesen Brief kaum, denn Mittwoch Mittag oder Donnerstag Mittag sehen wir uns in der Mühlgasse. Ich trau mich gar nicht zärtlich zu sein, nicht einmal im Briefe. Da Du es in Wirklichkeit jetzt nicht magst und Du so lebendig vor mir stehst, wenn ich Dir schreibe, muß ich mich zurückhalten. Aber glaube nur, daß ich

die süßesten Träume, auch im Wachen habe, ich liege vor Dir
und umfasse Deine Knie, ich streichle über Deine braune Haut
an verschwiegenen Stellen und ich bin collosal glücklich
darüber, daß ich Dich so gerne habe und Du mich auch ein
bischen und so lieb bist zu mir.

Herzliche Küße Dein Fritz.

(Vienna City Library, Manuscript Section I N 102.557)

11.   The Girardi episode that follows is adapted from Chapter III of
'When Vienna Was Vienna'.
12.   There is a clear indication in Irma Karczewska's reminiscences that at
the time of her first encounter with Kraus she had already had at least
one lover (*Notebook*, 12 November 1930). Irma's lovers included the
anarchist author Erich Mühsam, who was also a member of Kraus's
circle at that time.
13.   In a diary entry of 7 May 1911 Mühsam recalls that during 1906 Irma
was suffering from venereal disease. See Erich Mühsam, *Tagebücher
1910–1924* (Munich, 1994), p. 32.
14.   'So schafft man sich selber sein Haus-Nemesiserl zur Privat-
Marterey', Nestroy, *Frühere Verhältnisse*, scene vii.
15.   This diagnosis of the dilemma in which Irma Karczewska found
herself later in life is vividly confirmed by her own reminiscences. In
her fictive dialogue with Kraus she laments not simply that he has
abandoned her, but that the pleasures and privileges which she had
enjoyed as his mistress have rendered her incapable of coping with
the mundane demands of everyday existence. The solitary reference
to Wittels in the *Notebook* recalls that when he proposed to her,
Kraus discouraged her from marrying him. However, the news that
Wittels was about to settle with his wife in America is recorded with
considerable chagrin: 'soll ich da nicht verbittert sein' (*Notebook*, 26
January 1931).

Wittels claims that Kraus 'forced her to compete with downtown
whores'. Although the formulation is disrespectful, its truth cannot
be denied. Kraus, who never married, had a fondness for triangular
relationships which enabled him to enjoy the affections of two
women at the same time. The person with whom Irma Karczewska
felt particularly competitive was Kraus's lifelong companion Helene
Kann, who did indeed live 'downtown' (in Vienna's First District).
Karczewska's notebook is full of embittered references to his
enduring attachment to the financially privileged Kann. At an earlier
stage, however, it is clear that Karczewska and Kann had been on
friendly terms. The following summary, written prior to the
discovery of Karczewska's notebook, still seems plausible: 'We may
infer that for a number of years Helene Kann remained on amicable
terms with Irma. Each woman seems to have been assigned a clearly
defined role in Kraus's unorthodox domestic arrangements. Helene,
who had initially herself been a celebrated courtesan, evidently came
to play a more motherly role, ensuring that Kraus was never short of
feminine company [. . .] Irma's position was more like that of a

dependent child. A card which Kete Parsenow sent to Kraus in January 1924 sums the situation up suggestively: "How are things going with you and your family? You know who I mean".' (Edward Timms, 'The "Child-Woman"': Freud, Kraus, Wittels and Irma Karczewska', *Austrian Studies* 1 [Edinburgh, 1990], p. 93).

16. Her death occurred on 1 January 1933. According to Sophie Schick, Irma Karczewska's suicide was motivated by the fear that she was suffering from a terminal illness, probably cancer. Towards the end of her notebook there are indeed repeated references to fears that she may have to be operated for a tumour ('Geschwulst'). However, it is clear from the distraught tone of other entries that grief and anger at being deprived of Kraus's affection and support must have been contributory factors. At certain points she poignantly expresses the feeling that, just as he once gave her life, so now he is driving her towards death: 'Du hast ein *jetzt*, nicht mit 15 Jahren wertvolles Geschöpf, dem Du eigentlich das Leben gabst, den Todesstoß versetzt' (*Notebook*, 12 November 1930). The story of her life (in so far as it can be reconstructed) reveals the darker dimensions of the erotic subculture of turn-of-the-century Vienna. Irma seems to have been treated as a plaything by privileged males who enjoyed social, educational and financial advantages which she was denied. Kraus subsequently seems to have done his best to support her and encourage her to achieve greater independence. And he can scarcely be held responsible for the fact that all four of her marriages ended in failure. But the *Notebook* makes it clear that at the end of her life she felt overwhelmed by a sense of having been exploited and abandoned.

17. Wedekind himself played the role of Jack the Ripper in the production of *Die Büchse der Pandora* staged by Kraus in Vienna in May 1905.

6: *The Rupture*

1. 'Die Lustseuche', published in *Die Fackel* on 16 December 1907 (*F*, 238, 1–24). 'As Sancho Panza . . .': quoted in *F*, 238, 10.

2. The Adolf Loos episode which follows derives from Chapter III of 'When Vienna Was Vienna'.

3. Bessie Bruce (1886–1921), with whom Loos lived after his legal separation from his first wife Lina Loos in 1905.

4. 'Analysis of a Hysterical State of Confusion', a presentation by Wittels on 27 October 1909 which was praised by Freud as the work of someone likely to become 'a master of analysis' (*Minutes*, II, 282–9).

5. The essay 'Weibliche Attentäter', published in *Die Fackel* on 12 March 1908 (*F*, 246–7, 26–38), emphasizes that female assassins like Vera Sassulitsch carried out their attacks while wearing their finest clothes ('Festkleidung', p. 35). At the meeting of the Psychoanalytic

Society on 10 April 1907, Freud endorsed Wittels's view that it is 'suppressed eroticism that puts the weapon in the hands of these women' (*Minutes*, I, 164).

6. The clothes worn by Vera Zasulich (Sassulitsch) on that cold January morning in 1878 when she shot and wounded the tyrannical Tsarist prison governor, General Fyodor Trepov, were a necessary part of her strategem. She had to dress elegantly in order to gain admission to his office, and her voluminous cloak enabled her to conceal a revolver. The jury were so impressed by her idealistic motives that she was acquitted, and she subsequently escaped abroad. For further details see Vera Broido, *Apostles into Terrorists: Women and The Revolutionary Movement in the Russia of Alexander II* (London, 1978).

7. In her notebook Irma Karczewska recalls that Wittels did propose marriage to her, but that Kraus discouraged her from accepting him: 'Als W[ittels] mir einen Heiratsantrag machte, [. . .] sagtest Du: Du wirst doch nicht' (*Notebook*, 26 January 1931).

8. The final contribution by Wittels to appear in *Die Fackel*, the story 'Gottesurteil', appeared in the number dated 22 May 1908 (*F*, 254–5, 14–19). Wittels's father died of a stroke on 20 May.

9. This collection, which appeared in mid–October 1908 under the title *Alte Liebeshändel* (Love Affairs from Bygone Days), was issued by Kraus's publisher, Verlag Jahoda & Siegel. The number of *Die Fackel* dated 26 October 1908 (*F*, 263) announces on the inside front cover that it has just appeared.

10. The final story in *Alte Liebeshändel* has the ironic title 'Der heilige Lueger'.

11. *Die sexuelle Not* (Sexual Misery) by Dr. Fritz Wittels (Avicenna) bears the imprint 'Vienna and Leipzig 1909'. Copies were already in circulation by mid–November 1908, since Kraus alludes to the title page of this book in *Die Fackel* of 30 November (*F*, 266, 20). When it was discussed by the Vienna Psychoanalytic Society on 16 December 1908, Freud made the following comments:

> Wittels's book, which presents proposals for reform, stems from two different sources – from, so to say, a paternal and a maternal source. The first one, represented by the *Fackel*, goes part of the way with us in its assertion that the suppression of sexuality is the root of all evil. But we go further, and say: we liberate sexuality through our treatment, but not in order that man may from now on be dominated by sexuality, but in order to make a suppression possible – a rejection of the instincts under the guidance of a higher agency. The *Fackel* stands for 'living out' one's instinctual desires to the point of satiating them [ausleben]; we distinguish, however, between a pathological process of repression and one that is to be regarded as normal (*Minutes*, II, 89).

12. Freud, *SE*, 10, 5–149.

13. 'Ich bin nichts als ein Forscher, dem durch ein merkwürdiges Zusammentreffen eine besonders wichtige Feststellung geglückt ist.

Mein Verdienst an diesem Erfolg wird sich auf die Entfaltung einiger allerdings nicht häufig gepflegten Charaktereigenschaften wie Unabhängigkeit und Wahrheitsliebe einschränken' (letter of 8 February 1925 from Freud to Wittels, now in the Manuscript Division, Library of Congress).

14. Wittels is alluding to the hero of Sinclair Lewis's novel *Babbit* (1922), a satirical portrait of a complacent middle-aged American business-man. He draws a further parallel between Kraus's writings and the satirical essays which the American critic H. L. Mencken wrote for the *American Mercury* between 1924 and 1933. When Kraus in 1930 found himself described by a Canadian reviewer as 'a kind of Austrian Mencken', he emphatically repudiated the parallel (*F*, 845–6, 23–4).

15. 'Psychoanalyse ist jene Geisteskrankheit, für deren Therapie sie sich hält'. This aphorism was actually published in *Die Fackel* five years later, on 30 May 1913 (*F*, 376–7, 21).

16. It was not until the early 1920s, as a result of his analysis with Stekel, that Wittels acknowledged an unconscious homosexual component in his love-hatred for Kraus. This is indicated by the following passage from his biography of Freud, which clearly alludes to the Karczewska episode: 'The immense success of women who are ardently desired and greatly loved depends upon homosexual impulses in men. The hetaera-cult of our day is no less homosexual than was that of classical Greece. What a man loves in the hetaera is the other men who have lain and will lie in her arms. Since the homosexual impulse is unconscious, it cannot manifest itself in the form of direct love for another man' (*Sigmund Freud: His Personality, His Teaching, and His School*, p. 212).

17. The text of this letter, which must have been written in early or mid-November 1908, does not survive. This self-identification with Brutus is ironically set out in *Die Fackel* of 30 November 1908 (*F*, 266, 23).

18. Kraus's attack on the (unnamed) Wittels appeared under the title 'Persönliches' in *Die Fackel* of 30 November 1908 (*F*, 266, 14–28).

19. Wittels fails to mention that in the weeks preceding this attack he had in fact been trying to develop his career as a journalist by writing articles for the *Berliner Tageblatt* and the Munich magazine *März*. Kraus seems to have taken exception to the journalistic tone of articles by Wittels like 'Feuilletonisten' (*März*, 1 September 1908), 'Globetrotters' (*Berliner Tageblatt*, 18 September 1908), and 'Mein Diener' (*Berliner Tageblatt*, 24 October 1908).

20. Wittels may be overdramatizing his sense of isolation. It was during this same period, probably in 1908 or 1909, that he fell in love and married Yerta Pick, the daughter of a Prague psychiatrist. The marriage was shortlived, since Yerta died of leukaemia in 1913. For a vivid description of Yerta, dancing an exotic Oriental dance shortly before her death, see Rudolf von Urban, *Myself Not Least: A Confessional Autobiography of a Psychoanalyst* (London, 1958),

pp.112–15. A comment about the death of Yerta attributed to Kraus, which suggests that she was also in love with him, is recorded in Arthur Schnitzler's diary on 28 December 1915, after a conversation with Wittels: 'Kraus: Seine (W.s) Frau ist an Enttäuschung gestorben – ; – ich habe sie immer erwartet, – eigentlich hat sie ja mich geliebt, alles was W. ist, hat er ja von mir, etc.' ('Kraus: His [Wittels's] wife died of disillusionment – ; – I was always expecting her, – after all, it was really me that she loved, everything that W. is derives from me, etc.').

21. This is an overstatement. *Die Fackel* abounds in reflections on the activities of irresponsible writers and journalists, but there are only occasional specific references to Wittels, who is never again mentioned by name. In *Die Fackel* of 23 November 1910 (*F*, 311–12, 56) there is a reference to the forthcoming court case. In *Die Fackel* of 23 May 1918 (*F*, 484–93, 140) Kraus refers to the author of a hysterical *roman à clef*, whose feelings of 'love-hatred' led him to send Kraus 'love letters'.

22. This was presumably Wittels's father-in-law, Professor Arnold Pick (1851–1924), father of his first wife Yerta.

23. Wittels was hired by the Director of the sanatorium, Rudolf von Urbantschitsch, who was also a member of the Vienna Psychoanalytic Society. For further information about the sanatorium, see Rudolf von Urban, *Myself Not Least*.

24. Wittels was present at a pre-First World War meeting for the last time on 1 June 1910. His resignation is recorded on 5 October 1910: 'Dr. Fritz Wittels left the Society some time ago' (*Minutes*, III, 2).

25. When 'the Kraus affair' was placed on the agenda at a meeting of the Vienna Psychoanalytic Society on 14 April 1910 attended by Wittels, the discussion was introduced by Adler (*Minutes*, II, 473). Details of the discussion are not recorded.

7: *The Scandal*

1. It is ironic that Wittels, writing his memoirs for posterity, avoids mentioning Irma Karczewska by name, whereas in the first edition of his novel he had made so little effort to disguise the identity of his heroine Mizerl, a name all too similar to that of Irma (Irmerl).

2. Kraus initiated the court action in the name of Irma, who was by this date married to her first husband Haselhoff, and of Ludwig von Janikowski, who by that date was terminally ill.

3. The case against Wittels's publishers, which took place in Berlin between November 1910 and February 1911, was presented by Kraus's lawyer Hugo Heinemann, assisted by a Dr Roth. On 18 February 1911 the court decided in favour of the plaintiffs, Frau Irma Haselhoff-Lich and Ministerialrat Dr Ritter von Janikowski, and the sale of further copies of the incriminating novel was prohibited.

4. *Ezechiel der Zugereiste* was completely reset (this time in Latin type)

and republished in Vienna in 1911 by Huber & Lahme. Wittels made a number of changes to disguise the personal references, so as to forestall further legal action. For example, Mizerl is renamed 'Dorl', and the episode in Venice about the broken heel becomes a quarrel about a torn dress. Since the Berlin court decided that the references to Janikowski (thinly disguised as the pretentious Polish intellectual Sinepopowski) were also defamatory, the name of this character is altered to Boris Popow and he becomes a Bulgarian.

5. The letters from Wittels to Freud were destroyed in Vienna in 1938, when the possessions of the Freud family were being packed up for the journey to London and it became clear that only a fraction of his vast correspondence could be preserved. See Anna Freud's letter of 15 December 1951 to Wittels's widow, Poldi Goetz Wittels (Collection of Gerhard Fichtner, Tübingen).

6. Comparison with the German original of this letter, which is now in the Library of Congress, shows that Wittels's translation is accurate. The only significant deviation is that Wittels uses the words 'affectionate letters' for Freud's more emotionally charged phrase 'zärtlich werbende Briefe'.

7. Wittels fails to mention the fourth book which he published during this period, *Über den Tod und über den Glauben an Gott* (Vienna, 1914), reflections on love, death and religious faith, dedicated to the memory of his wife Yerta.

8: Reconciliation

1. During the First World War Wittels served as an army doctor, first on the Eastern Front, later in Turkey, Syria and Palestine, where he was attached to an Austrian medical mission led by Rudolf von Urbantschitsch. His experiences prompted him to write the satirical novel *Zacharias Pamperl oder der verschobene Halbmond* (Vienna, 1923). It was these war experiences that led him to abandon his youthful individualism and become a socialist and a pacifist. In Grodek he had witnessed the execution of Ruthenian dissidents by the Habsburg army (*An End to Poverty*, p.205), while his experiences in Turkey led him to include a graphic account of the Armenian genocide in *Zacharias Pamperl*.

Despite the horrors witnessed as an army doctor, Wittels did not lose his sense of humour, as is clear from a characteristic episode recounted by his son: 'When the British attack finally came, Fritz was busy at the hospital tending the wounded. After some thirty hours of battle, when no one got any sleep, there was a lull and Fritz decided to lie down and get some rest. When he woke up, the tide of battle had turned and the British forces had overrun the Austrian field hospital. He came out, and there were only English orderlies and doctors – all the Austrian personnel had fled. Since he was even then able to speak fluent English, he got on well with the "enemy" personnel and continued to tend the Austrian wounded, while they cared for the British wounded. As the tide of battle reversed and the British were driven back into the sea, the Austrian and Turkish forces recaptured the hospital. When the British evacuated, they left Fritz in charge of the wounded who had been left behind, both English and Austrian. The net effect was that he remained the only Austrian who had not fled his post. For this he was awarded the Iron Cross, Second Class' (letter of 14 July 1988 from John R. Wittels to Edward Timms).

2. On his return to Vienna in 1919, after his release from a prisoner-of-war camp, Wittels became actively involved in politics. He joined the Verein Allgemeine Nährpflicht, an organization which campaigned for a fairer distribution of wealth, inspired by the ideas of Joseph Popper-Lynkeus. During 1919 he also wrote a series of articles for the left-wing newspaper *Der Abend*, expressing impatience with the cautious policies of the Austrian Social Democrats and calling for more radical action.

3. Wittels's account of Stekel's abilities provides a corrective to the negative picture which predominates in conventional histories of psychoanalysis. During the early 1920s Stekel was in a very productive phase, developing new techniques of short-term ('active') psychoanalysis and even establishing his own international association, the Organisation 'der unabhängigen ärztlichen Analytiker'.

4. Wittels omits to mention that in this same period he himself had become a father. In 1920 he married his second wife, Lilly Krishaber, and in 1922 his son Hans Rudolf (John R. Wittels) was born.

5. According to the *Autobiography of Wilhelm Stekel* (New York, 1950, p. 230), Wittels presented a copy of the German edition of his Freud biography to Stekel with the inscription: 'Not one line of this book could have been written without your help.'

6. In fact, the marginal annotations in Freud's copy, now in the Freud Museum in London, indicate that certain passages greatly annoyed him, particularly Wittels's positive assessment of Stekel. A marginal comment in Freud's handwriting on page 47 reads: 'Zuviel Stekel' ('Too much Stekel').

7. A more complete English translation of this letter, including the hostile comments on Stekel, can be found in *Letters of Sigmund Freud 1873–1939* (London, 1961), pp. 350–52.

8. It was probably at Wittels's suggestion that Stekel on 22 January 1924 wrote a letter to Freud (now in the Library of Congress) suggesting that they should meet and emphasizing that his own group of sixty independent analysts were not hostile to the Freudians: 'Wir stehen alle auf dem Boden von Freud. Deshalb wäre ein paralleles Arbeiten und Kämpfen gegen die Gegner und Verwässerer der Analyse möglich' ('We all stand on the foundation of Freud. Thus we could work together and campaign against the opponents and diluters of psychoanalysis.') The offer was ignored.

9. In the standard English translation of 'On the History of the

Psycho–Analytic Movement' the passage reads: 'Stekel, who at first did such very creditable work but afterwards went totally astray' (*SE*, 14, 19).

10.   The German text of this letter (Manuscript Division, Library of Congress) reads as follows:

> Wien IX., Berggasse 19
> 4. 1. 24
>
> Geehrter Herr Doktor
>   Ich wollte Ihnen gerne einen Gefallen thun. Natürlich konnte ich meine Kritik an St. nicht unterdrücken, noch weniger mich in einer Weise über ihn äußern, die mit seiner Selbsteinschätzung zusammenstimmt. Aber wenn der Ersatz eines harten Wortes durch eine mildere Wendung seine Kränkung verringern u ihn selbst zum Gebrauch höflicherer Umgangsformen bewegen kann, so möchte ich dem nicht im Wege sein.
>   Ich erkundigte mich also noch am Tage, da ich Ihren Brief erhielt, wie es mit dem Druck des Aufsatzes 'Zur Geschichte der Psa Bewegung' stände, und erfuhr, daß nichts mehr zu machen sei. Der Druck war vollendet und die Bogen bereits beim Buchbinder. Es muß also alles bleiben wie es ist.
>   Mit ergebenem Gruß
>   Ihr Freud

11.   Their first meeting for fifteen years took place on 4 March 1925. A diary entry in a black notebook marked 'Begonnen im November 1913', now in the Brill Library, records the evening spent with Freud as follows: 'Mittwoch, 4. III. 1925, ½ 9 abends über Einladung bei Prof. Freud post quindecim annos'.

12.   The German original of this remark, as recorded in the same black notebook, reads as follows: 'Ich habe zwei Verbrechen begangen: daß ich auf das Cocain aufmerksam gemacht und daß ich den Stekel zur Psychoanalyse geführt habe.' This is followed by further denigratory comments on Stekel.

13.   Freud himself recommended his readmission because (as the editors of the *Minutes* explain) he 'was fond of Wittels and valued his wealth of ideas' (*Minutes*, I, xxxvii).

14.   The original German text of these two letters, now in the Manuscript Division, Library of Congress, reads as follows:

> (Villa Schüler) Semmering, 31. Juli 1927
>
> Lieber Herr Doktor
>   Sie werden sich vielleicht wundern, daß ich Sie um eine literarische Gefälligkeit bitte, aber Sie werden mich gewiß bald verstanden haben. Ich habe in diesen letzten Jahren mehrere Analysen von Fetischismus anstellen können u. dabei jedesmal eine überraschend einfache Lösung gefunden. Diese will ich nun zum Gegenstand einer kleinen Mitteilung machen. Es gibt aber

jemand, der ein dickes Buch über den Gegenstand geschrieben hat. Nach allen Regeln des wissenschaftlichen Betriebs sollte ich das Buch lesen u. mir wenigstens die Sicherheit holen, daß der findige jemand nicht schon meine Lösung gefunden hat, so wenig wahrscheinlich dies auch sein mag. Allein – ich bringe mich nicht dazu, kann einen inneren Widerstand von der Art eines Reinlichkeitsinstinktes nicht über-winden. Ich weiß schon, daß dies nicht recht ist, aber im Alter wird man leicht absonderlich und sucht seinen Eigensinn festzuhalten.

Was ich an Ihrer Vergangenheit sonst so sehr bedauere wird mir diesmal verwertbar. Sie kennen gewiß das Buch von Stekel über den Fetischismus. Läßt es sich machen, daß Sie mir in wenigen Sätzen angeben, zu welchem Ergebnis dieser Autor über die Natur u. Absicht des Fetisch kommt? Die Bitte besteht natürlich nur für den Fall, daß er ein solches Ergebnis ausspricht und daß es Ihnen nicht zu beschwerlich wird, es herauszuschälen, im anderen Falle sagen Sie mir auf einer Postkarte ab; in jedem Falle schweigen Sie aber gefälligst über dies Eingeständnis meiner Idiosynkrasie, die ich mir schwer erworben habe.

Mit herzlichem Gruß
Ihr Freud

Semmering, 8.8.27

Lieber Herr Doktor
Ich danke Ihnen sehr. Sie haben mir einen guten Dienst geleistet und meine Publikation erst ermöglicht. Ich will Ihnen dafür gerne verraten – aber behalten Sie es für sich, daß der Fetisch nichts zehnfaches sondern etwas recht einfaches ist, nämlich der Ersatz für den einst geglaubten und so hoch eingeschätzten Penis des Weibes (der Mutter), also eine Schöpfung des Trotzes gegen die Kastration und ein Schutz gegen die Homosexualität.

Mit herzlichem Gruß
Ihr Freud

15   *SE*, 21, 149–57.

9:   *America: Making Amends*

1. Wittels first went to New York at the invitation of Alvin Johnson to give lectures at the New School for Social Research.
2. In the German original the section of the letter quoted by Wittels reads as follows:

    Wien IX, Berggasse 19
    20.4.1928

    Lieber Herr Doktor
    Mein Rat ist eindeutig. Wenn Sie Anknüpfungen in den U S

haben, Aussicht dort durch Lehren and Analysieren gut zu erwerben, so versäumen Sie es nicht, hinüberzugehen u. die Gelegenheit auszunützen. Sie kennen die trostlosen materiellen Zustände in Wien und die Unwahrscheinlichkeit einer baldigen Änderung. Die Sorge um den Lebensunterhalt thut auch dem Charakter nicht gut.

Ihre Nebenabsicht dort Adler zur bekämpfen ist natürlich sehr lobenswert. Legen Sie nicht den Hauptakzent darauf, denn diese seichte Abbreviatur der Analyse muß den Amerikanern durch ihren positiven Gehalt wie durch das, was sie verleugnet, sehr gut passen. Aber Amerika ist so groß, weit und urteilslos, daß dort Platz für alle Gegensätze nebeneinander ist . . .

Indem ich Ihnen ausgiebigen Erfolg wünsche
Ihr Freud

The full German text of this letter is in the Library of Congress, which possesses originals or photocopies of seven letters from Freud to Wittels, some of which are 'restricted until 2000' (letter of 1 November 1988 from David Wigdor, Assistant Chief of the Manuscript Division, to Edward Timms).

3. The German original of Freud's letter to Wittels of 11 July 1928 is not available. The German text of his letter of 7 August 1928 reads as follows:

> Semmering, 7.8.1928
>
> Lieber Herr Doktor
> Gewiß, der Amerikaner und die Psychoanalyse, das paßt oft so wenig zusammen, daß man an Grabbe's Vergleich erinnert wird, wie wenn ein Rabe "ein weißes Hemd anzieht." Woran das liegt, ist noch nicht aufgeklärt worden. Vielleicht bringen Sie es heraus; sicher ist aber, daß Sie den Amerikaner nicht ändern werden. Am besten ist es, man hält sich reserviert auf dem Sokel seiner Wissenschaft und läßt Personen wie Ereignisse an sich herankommen.
> Mit besten Reisewünschen
> Ihr Freud

4. During his first visit to New York in 1928 Wittels was invited to give a paper to the New York Psychoanalytic Society, and in March 1932 he was admitted to membership of the society by transfer from Vienna. Initially, his wife and son had spent part of their time in Austria, but by the mid-1930s the family was permanently settled in the United States. Wittels became a member of the American Psychoanalytic Society and the American Psychiatric Association. In addition to lecturing at the New School, he became an instructor at the New York Psychoanalytic Institute, and he also worked as a research fellow at Bellevue Hospital, New York University, and as associate psychoanalyst at Columbia University. In 1940 he was naturalized and became an American citizen. An obituary tribute by

Philip R. Lehrman, published in the *Psychoanalytic Quarterly* in 1951, records that even in his final years 'Wittels radiated the enthusiasm of youth'. His second marriage ended in divorce, and in 1947 he married as his third wife his former nurse, Poldi Goetz.

5. The original text of Freud's letter of 11 November 1928 (Manuscripts Division, Library of Congress) has been compressed at certain points in Wittel's translation:

Wien IX, Berggasse 19
11.XI.1928

Lieber Herr Doktor
    Ihren inhaltsreichen, eigentümlich verhaltenen, illusionsfreien Brief erhalten und mit Befriedigung gelesen. Es ist mir eine große Beruhigung – vielleicht haben Sie an den Ernst meiner Teilnahme doch nicht geglaubt – zu hören, daß Ihnen die materielle Absicht Ihrer Amerikareise gesichert scheint. Ihre Urteile über Personen und Verhältnisse erscheinen mir sämtlich richtig. Es sind dort keine Analytiker in unserem Sinne, sondern Psychiater, die sich der Analyse bedienen. Alle kulturellen Perspektiven entfallen für sie, daran können wir nichts ändern. Brill wird sein Ziel nicht erreichen, Sie sehen es richtig vorher. Bei Schmalhausen hatte ich mich ausnahmsweise zu einem groben Brief hinreißen lassen auf eine dumme Antwort seinerseits habe ich nicht weiter reagiert. Eine gewisse Mischung von ignorance and irreverence ist für amerikan Arbeiten charakteristisch. Auf wissenschaftliche Beiträge haben wir von dort nicht zu rechnen sowenig wie auf Geldmittel für unsere gemeinnützige Zwecke.
    Sie haben sehr klug daran gethan, Anstoß zu vermeiden und denen, die vielleicht nach Ihnen kommen, die Schwierigkeiten nicht zu vergrößern. Wenn ich einige einführende Worte für Sie sagen soll, so kann es nur geschehen, wenn Sie mich wissen lassen, was Sie haben wollen, es mir gewissermaßen vorschreiben.
    Was Sie über das Abklingen der Adlerei sagen, hat mich doch überrascht. Ich hätte geglaubt, eine so seichte Vereinfachung schwerer Probleme würde sich gerade dem amerik. Geist besondern empfehlen, etwa wie der Behaviorism. Es ist wohl nicht zu übersehen, daß der Amerikaner auch in der Wissenschaft von seinen politischen Leidenschaften beherrscht wird. Also Monroe-Doktrin – der alte Mann Europa hat nichts dreinzureden u muß klein gemacht werden. Wahrscheinlich das psycho-logische Hauptmotiv für Amerikas Eingreifen in den Krieg.
    Ich war unterdessen in Berlin u habe mir von Prof. Schröder eine Prothese machen lassen, mit der das Leben besser erträglich ist, ohne darum eitel behagen zu sein.
    In Erwartung Ihrer weiteren Nachrichten, mit besten Wünschen für Ihren Erfolg
        Ihr Freud

The German text of subsequent letters from Freud cited by Wittels is not available.

6. '"Das habe ich getan", sagt mein Gedächtnis. "Das kann ich nicht getan haben" – sagt mein Stolz und bleibt unerbittlich. Endlich – gibt das Gedächtnis nach.' Nietzsche, *Beyond Good and Evil*, 1886, Part Four, para. 68.

7. The full text of Wittels's retraction appeared under the title 'Revision of a Biography' in *Psychoanalytical Review*, 20 (1933), pp. 361–74.

10: Freud in America

1. Wittels is referring to the controversies within the New York Psychoanalytic Society provoked by radical new theories which diverged from the orthodox teachings of Freud, including the ego psychology of Heinz Hartmann and the feminist critique initiated by Karen Horney's *New Ways in Psychoanalysis* (1939). Thus around 1940 he found himself in the unfamiliar role of defender of the establishment.

2. 'Denn wie das Wasser, das durch ein Schiff verdrängt wird, gleich hinter ihm wieder zusammenstürzt, so schließt sich auch der Irrtum, wenn vorzügliche Geister ihn beiseitegedrängt und sich Platz gemacht haben, hinter ihnen geschwind wieder naturgemäß zusammen' (Goethe, *Dichtung und Wahrheit*, Part III, Book 15).

3. In *New Ways in Psychoanalysis* Horney had directly challenged Freud's libido theory and his emphasis on the primacy of the instincts. Wittels's reaction took the form of an open letter dated 13 March 1940, circulated to fellow members of the New York Psychoanalytic Society, denouncing Horney for denying 'that our sex life is of fundamental importance in the structure of human psychology'. Disregarding Horney's attempts at finer discrimination, he insists that the issue is 'Freud or no Freud'. The Psychoanalytic Society was experiencing a dramatic increase in student numbers, and Wittels, supported by other senior members of the Education Committee like Lawrence Kubie, was determined to prevent Horney's new approach from gaining too much influence on the teaching programme: 'Our students come to us because of Freud's invulnerable name expecting to be taught the result of forty years of patient psychoanalytic work. Instead, we are urgently asked to teach them a doctrine diametrically opposed to Freud's findings and rejected by probably ninety-nine per cent of the experienced members of the International Psychoanalytic Association.' A year later, after protracted in-fighting, the faction led by Wittels and Kubie succeeded in depriving Horney of her status as instructor. This provoked her into resigning from the New York Psychoanalytic Society in April 1941 and setting up her own rival group, the Association for the Advancement of Psychoanalysis. For a more detailed account of Wittels's involvement in these controversies, see Susan Quinn, *A Mind of her Own: The Life of Karen*

Horney (London, 1987).

4. The 'typically American doctrines' ironized in this passage also made a considerable impact in Europe, not least the crusade for 'Moral Rearmament' led by Frank Buchman (1878–1961).

5. Wittels's feeling that the popularity of the pragmatic techniques of behaviourism consitituted a serious barrier to the reception of psychoanalysis was shared by Freud himself. In conversation with the American author Max Eastman, Freud is reported to have said: 'Perhaps you're a behaviourist. According to your John B. Watson, even consciousness doesn't exist. But that's just silly. That's nonsense. Consciousness exists quite obviously and everywhere – except perhaps in America' (quoted in Ronald W. Clark, *Freud, the Man and the Cause*, London, 1980, p. 429).

6. *Moses and Monotheism* (1939), *SE*, 23, 7–137.

Index of Names

This index lists the names mentioned by Wittels in his memoirs. It does not cover the further references in the commentary. Dates of birth and death are given as known, but in some cases complete identification has not been possible.